W9-DJJ-530

HEDDA STERNE ***No. 32***

AMERICAN PAINTING TODAY

EDITED BY

NATHANIEL POUSETTE-DART

HASTINGS HOUSE, PUBLISHERS, NEW YORK

LOREN MacIVER ***Spatters and Leaves***

The color reproductions were printed from plates generously made available by the following:

Grace Borgenicht Gallery	*Invocation* by Samuel Adler (jacket illustration)
The Art Galleries, The University of California at Los Angeles	*Sunset* by John Marin
Collection of Mrs. Edith Gregor Halpert, Courtesy of the Downtown Gallery	
Collection of the Whitney Museum of American Art, New York	*Betrothal II* by Arshile Gorky
Arts Magazine Courtesy of Frank K. M. Rehn Gallery	*The Summertime* by Morris Kantor
Arts Magazine Courtesy of The Brooklyn Museum	*Abstract No. 1* by Louis Shanker

Library of Congress Catalog Card Number: 56-10969

Published simultaneously in Canada
by S. J. Reginald Saunders, Publishers, Toronto 1

Printed in the United States of America

CONTENTS

THE ADVISORY COMMITTEE 6

FOREWORD 7

INTRODUCTION: A Brief Resume of Some of the Experiments, Developments and Influences in Contemporary Art 9

PAINTINGS 16-32

THE ARTIST AS CRITIC *by Nathaniel Pousette-Dart* 33

PAINTINGS 36-83

PERMANENT OPINIONS: Yesterday and Today 84

PAINTINGS 86-114

ART REFERENCE BRIEFS:

National Artists Organizations 116

National Art Organizations 118

Art Periodicals 119

Suggested Reading, compiled by Muriel Baldwin 122

REFERENCE INDEX AND CREDITS:

Artists, Galleries, Museums, Collectors 124

HENRY RASMUSSEN *Involution in a Rocker*

Advisory Committee

Selections of work for reproduction in this book have been made by an Advisory Committee consisting of the following museum directors and curators.*

Hermon More, *Chairman*
Director
Whitney Museum of American Art
New York, N. Y.

H. Harvard Arnason
Director
Walker Art Center
Minneapolis, Minn.

James S. Byrnes
Curator of Contemporary and Modern Art
Los Angeles County Museum
Los Angeles, Calif.

Leslie Cheek, Jr.
Director
Virginia Museum of Fine Arts
Richmond, Va.

D. S. Defenbacher
Director
Forth Worth Art Museum
Forth Worth, Tex.

Joseph T. Fraser, Jr.
Director
Pennsylvania Academy of the Fine Arts
Philadelphia, Pa.

Richard E. Fuller
President and Director
Seattle Art Museum
Seattle, Wash.

Una E. Johnson
Curator, Prints and Drawings
Brooklyn Museum
Brooklyn, N. Y.

William M. Milliken
Director
Cleveland Museum of Art
Cleveland, Ohio

Dr. Grace L. McCann Morley
Director
San Francisco Museum of Art
San Francisco, Calif.

Perry T. Rathbone
Director
City Art Museum of St. Louis
St. Louis, Mo.

Andrew C. Ritchie
Director, Department of Painting and Sculpture
Museum of Modern Art
New York, N. Y.

Frederick A. Sweet
Curator of American Painting and Sculpture
The Art Institute of Chicago
Chicago, Ill.

Frederick S. Wight
Director of the Art Galleries,
The University of California at Los Angeles
Formerly, The Institute of Contemporary Art
Boston, Mass.

* The Advisory Committee is not responsible for the reproduction or arrangement of the paintings as shown in this book or for any of the editorial ideas herein expressed.

FOREWORD

> Continuity: emergence: creativity — these are the basic postulates of the new synthesis.
>
> LEWIS MUMFORD

Every book which has an innate significance, seems simple — because hard work and inspiration have eliminated all unessential material. The idea for this book was an outgrowth of many dynamic discussions held by the Artists for Victory, during World War II. One of these discussions gave rise to a plan to help the creative artists in this country to recognition. It was this concept of awakening the public to the high quality of the work of our artists which gave rise to the idea of a *Library of Creative American Art,* initiated by this volume.

It was not the intent in such a library to establish what might be called an "American Style" inasmuch as style at its best, is an unconscious quality springing from the beliefs and emotional responses of the individual artist. Indeed, the whole world of today is a source of inspiration to the creative artist. He may be influenced by American Colonial art, by the modern developments in Europe, by Primitive Negro sculpture, by the art of the South Sea Islands or the paintings of India, Iran or Japan. Thus, the paintings reproduced here cover a wide range of expression — from the sincere realism of John Sloan to the so-called pure abstractionism of Joseph Albers.

In selecting work for reproduction in this book, it was decided that a committee of eminent Museum Directors from many sections of the country would be best qualified to make intelligent choices. This decision was in harmony with what a well-known Chicago critic once said, "It is for the museum to hunt out the new talent and to invite it, on the basis of a catholic taste and rigorous standards . . . The excellent, in the deepest meaning of that word, is what we are after in speaking of new talent; it will never be found by mass methods." However, since no selection of art by any "jury" or similar group, however able its members, can ever be wholly objective, the controversial nature of our selections must be recognized as well as the fact that the work of certain deserving artists may very well have been overlooked.

Throughout the ages art has undergone continual change, so it is not safe to become too set in one's opinions. Nevertheless, it would be well to try to distinguish between that art which is fundamentally sincere and profound, and that which is tricky, clever, or merely superficial.

True comprehension of art comes from a genuine interest, serious study and a corresponding grasp of each picture's intent and inner meaning. Only in this way can one hope to absorb the beauty of its creation and expression.

The creative artist is described in these words by Dr. James A. Diefenbeck, Professor of Philosophy at the University of Illinois: "His work (the artist), as long as he remains true to his vocation, is done primarily for himself and represents an effort to clarify and crystalize his feeling, to order and portray inner emotions in an objective form, so that they become explicit and understandable. He seeks to express the reality of an apprehension of life by at once creating and clarifying the feelings and emotions which are entwined with it."

Sincere thanks are extended to the many individuals and organizations who have assisted in the arduous task of preparing this work for publication.

Without the enthusiastic and invaluable help of my wife, and her belief in the validity of the original idea, this book would never have appeared.

My friend, Marjorie Bell, has given generously of her time and talent. Many of the reproductions for the selections by our Committee of Museum Directors were procured by her. She is largely responsible for the reference section and, in addition, she supplied many valuable ideas and suggestions throughout.

To Miss Muriel Baldwin, until recently Chief of the Art and Architecture Division of the New York Public Library, sincere thanks are due for the compilation of the *Suggested Reading List,* a compact source of inspiration and information.

Hermon More, Director of the Whitney Museum of American Art, and Chairman of our Advisory Committee, cooperated generously and provided invaluable assistance over a long period, ever since the initial planning stages of the book. And to all the members of Mr. More's Committee, may we express our deep appreciation of their interest and help.

I owe a debt of gratitude to gallery directors throughout the country for their generous participation in the project. And, most of all, thanks are due to the artists themselves . . . both those whose work is here reproduced and the many others for whose work there was no space in this initial volume.

NATHANIEL POUSETTE-DART

INTRODUCTION

A brief résumé of some of the experiments, developments and influences in CONTEMPORARY ART

"The future of Art is no longer linked definitely with the success of this or that group. We should seek rather to mirror the results of this widespread activity and grasp its fundamental basis."
—from an editorial in L'Amour De L'Art

THE IMPACT of the Armory Exhibition in 1913 made the American public conscious that "time was marching on" and that new widespread activities following in the wake of scientific, political and artistic developments were giving the art of the twentieth century a new face and a different inner character.

In 1886, in an exhibition in Paris led by Manet and Monet, Impressionism was established. Some years before, Delacroix had said, "Let us banish from our palette all earth colors; keep the brush-strokes distinct, not fused, and thus secure energy and freshness; the greater the opposition in color, the greater the brilliance." The Impressionists based the tenets of their philosophy on his ideas. They believed in creating an illusion of light and atmosphere in the subjects they painted. To paint objects enveloped in light became not only an artistic problem, but a scientific one as well. And so it was that color scientists like Helmholtz and Chevreul took a very active part in this movement. Monet sometimes painted as many as twenty versions of the same subject in order to discover how it was affected by different lighting. This he did by painting it from the same position, but at different times of the day.

Georges Seurat and Paul Signac of the Pointillist school carried the theory of pure color-juxtaposition and -harmony to greater scientific levels of precision. They painted their pictures with tiny roundish spots of equal size — but they were influenced by the structure in the work of Paolo Uccello and Piero della Francesca. Their basically intellectual yet sensitive approach produced paintings which were frozen into effective patterns by a delicate, machine-like technique. With these painters line-direction was a passion, as was line-relationship.

Georges Seurat together with Cezanne, Van Gogh and Gauguin belonged to the group of painters who were loosely styled Post-Impressionists. All of these artists had their influence on the development of modern art.

Cezanne, using nature as a means of achieving organizational ends, declared that all objects in nature might be resolved into significant type-forms — such as cones, cylinders, and cubes. This concrete concept helped to give his work a classical architectural structure. This was not attained by the use of a single design-formula but by an intuitive acceptance of the "good Gestalt" principle which demanded of him absolute perfection in unifying all of his aesthetic elements. In contemplating his paintings one becomes conscious that they are all predicated on a simple triangular construction. Sometimes, as in the "Card Players" and the portrait of Madame Cezanne, the base of the triangle is at the bottom of the picture; sometimes it drives in from either the right or the left side.

Van Gogh, with his intensely human approach, gave a new shape and character to the juxtaposed colors of the Impressionists. His style fused the expressionism of Delacroix, the earthiness absorbed from Millet's work and the design patterns derived from Japanese prints. This style led naturally to Expressionism as practised by Kokoschka, Munch, Nölde and Soutine. Expressionism in Germany was in direct contrast to the work being produced by the scientifically-minded artists of the period. Oskar Kokoschka crucified his keen intelligence when he created an art dominated by dynamic emotion.

Gauguin, intrigued by the bizarre tendencies in the work of some of his contemporaries, began boldly to copy their styles and techniques. But it was the nostalgic and decorative art of the South Sea Islands which finally satisfied his craving for savage mysticism. Disagreeing with Cezanne's belief that color and form should be one, he treated color as a thing in itself and made it function as a decorative vehicle. Cezanne said, "Gauguin is not a painter — he only makes Chinese images." Gauguin's retort was, "Keep the Persians, the Cambodians and a bit of the Egyptians in mind."

Picasso, from the very first, was an adventurer. He proceeded in a straight line, or rather in a series of straight lines. At first, seeking to find his own metier, he absorbed the essential qualities in the work of Puvis de Chavanne, Pisarro, Gauguin, Lautrec and others among his contemporaries. But it was only after he started to absorb the arts of the past — of Spain, Greece, Italy, Africa — that he developed his particular power to re-create and expand the perimeters of today's expression.

Picasso's handwriting shows his great versatility. It betrays his earthiness, his tremendous self-confidence and his dictatorial will. He conceives of himself as the greatest creator of the universe. In a sense, Picasso seems to have no memory, for each one of his creative phases is a new and distinct world wherein he absorbs and re-creates the work of past cultures. He is his own hero. His will to power dominates him and makes of him a great assimilator and creator.

Making use of Cezanne's magnificent plane relationships, of the powerful form in Negro sculpture and of the masterful deep-space compositions in Chinese painting, Picasso and Braque began the experiments which led to Cubism.

The Cubists upset the time-honored tradition that a picture should be painted from one static position. On one canvas they painted their figures from many angles. This caused their canvases to take on a feeling of abstraction. In this one major step they freed the artist from a too-great dependence on nature and made art a pure expression like the music of Mozart or Bach.

The newly-awakened interest in Negro sculpture brought an awareness of the magical way in which these primitive artists used several kinds of material to produce an authentic beauty. Selecting from a wealth of weird and mysterious materials such as hair, metals, rope, wood and stones, they produced works later styled collages and montages.

Inspired by these works, Picasso, Braque, Gris and Gleizes began to experiment with extra-plastic materials such as newspapers, clippings, pieces of wood, glass, string, bone, cement, sand, and others, pasting them onto their canvases. These adventures led other artists to go still further and try to achieve structural and architectural qualities in their work by adding all sorts of unrelated objects, such as household appliances, rat traps, pieces of discarded machinery, and so on. Lipschitz and Laurens, stimulated by these experiments, made paintings with cement. An added impetus was given to these experiments when Picasso collected an assortment of old boards, assembled them in a frame and called the result a Construction.

In Russia, Malevich, Gabo, Pevsner and Tatlin launched the Suprematist movement, examples of which seem to have more in common with architecture than with painting. After the Revolution Gabo and Pevsner left Russia and started a new stylized art movement which they called Constructivism.

In England, Wyndham Lewis instigated a movement called Vorticism, the principal exponent of which was Gaudier Breszka. Breszka's fame was achieved through a very enthusiastic book about him and his work by Ezra Pound. Breszka, inspired by the work of Chinese jade- and stone-carvers, attained an expressive completeness of organization in his intense creations. Unfortunately his fervent convictions and ideals ended in the trenches of France during the first World War. On the butt of his rifle he inscribed a powerfully concise outline of his philosophy of art.

The work of Odilon Redon, that of the Dutch painters Peter Brueghel and Hieronymos Bosch, and the etchings of Goya, together with the ideas of Freud and his precursors, were doubtless responsible for the dramatic and sensational ideas which led to the formation of the Surrealist movement. Dali, the most publicized artist of this group, is a most skilful technician and an artist of considerable merit—but he lost caste with his contemporaries when he stooped to sensational dramatics and to fashion and commercialism. Attempts to startle and mystify the beholder, through combining the animate and the inanimate as they have never before been combined, have very little aesthetic value per se. When their novelty wears off, they become tiresome.

The Futurists, practising aesthetic automatism, were violently antagonistic to the art of the Fauves (that of Matisse in particular), which fostered the ideas of purity, balance and serenity. Boccioni, Giancomo Balla, Gino Severini and the poet Marinetti were active adherents of Futurism. Dominated by ideas of conquest and expansion, they sought to express in their work movement and the passage of time. Boccioni strove for a new dynamism. He felt that the artist must consciously search his subject for the lines which would give his painting the greatest dynamic power. The Futurists, in their attempt to express time, often turned their paintings into fantastic illustrations more suited to the cinema than to painting.

The aftermath of the first World War brought disillusionment to many. In Zurich, on February 8th, 1916, a group of artists gathered in the Cabaret Voltaire to form a new art organization. With the assistance of a paper knife plunged at random into a French dictionary, they picked a name for their "ism" which turned out to be wildly appropriate. The name was "Dada", meaning "Hobby-horse."

The adherents of this new Dadaism rejected inividualism as narrow and prescribed; they were in favor of communal activity. At first they took some of their ideas from the Surrealists and the Futurists. But it was not very long before they turned on these two groups and attempted in every possible way to destroy everything for which they stood. Their principal idea was to ridicule everything which was conventionally accepted. By means of ridiculous juxtapositions, vulgarities of all kinds, childish pranks and fantasies, they hoped to shock and anger everybody. Although they were in revolt against the "good Gestalt" of Cezanne, it is interesting to note that the only portion of their work which has any real aesthetic value today bears the imprint of tradition. This is true of the work of Duchamp, Picabia, Tzara, Huelsenbeck, Archipenko and Arp.

When the Dada group was first formed, Hans Arp was one of its leading spirits, but later he broke away from it. He believed that an object such as a stone was extremely important because it was "a sign of order", an evidence that we must continually return to the fountain-head of creativity. Although extreme simplicity was the key-note of his own work, he felt that multiplicity most fully expressed the dynamic spirit of our times.

The Bauhaus movement in Germany was started by a group of self-taught men whose primary interest was in architecture. Many of their ideas derived from Surrealism and Dadaism had been tempered to fit their philosophy which stressed technical progress. Believing as they did that *every one* was talented, they were not particularly interested in genius.

They were staunch believers in Sullivan's edict that "form follows function"; and their adherents endorsed the theories of Neoplasticism, Suprematism and Constructivism. The Bauhaus movement has widely influenced architecture and the arts of painting, publishing and advertising. Mondrian, Klee and Kandinsky, all of whom were associated with the Bauhaus group, have exerted a strong influence on the development of modern painting.

Mondrian, with his keen intellectual sensitivity, gave a new valuation to absolute relationships in space and design. He laid special emphasis on the pleasure derived from the formal elements in art and on our instinctive response to coordinated patterns.

Kandinsky, from his earliest period wherein he worked from nature, to his latest one wherein he tried to do pure non-objective painting, was a very significant and creative artist. Although he believed that during his last phase he had freed himself completely from all nature influence, actually he had merely transferred his interest from life on earth to life in the heavens. Instead of trees, plants and landscapes, he directed his interest to stars, moons and the worlds of outer space.

Paul Zucker has said, "The content is as decisive in a work of art as form. Indeed, form and content are so interlinked in all great works of art that separating them might lead to artificial distortions." Is this the reason why Rudolf Bauer's work and that of Moholy-Nagy fall far short of Kandinsky's? When the intellect is in the saddle, art seems to disappear.

For art, like life, undergoes continual change. It is of vital importance to keep the periphery of each newly-emerging movement from solidifying —because, as Sheldon Cheney once said, "Theorizing begins when creative energy has run thin." New aspects of the laws of aesthetics are being discovered continually, but the fundamental principles of creative art remain the same. That is why a great piece of Chinese sculpture, a Negro wood carving, an El Greco painting and a landscape by Cezanne can exist happily together. Perhaps that is why Picasso said, "To me there is no past or future in art. If a work cannot live always in the present, it must not be considered at all."

NATHANIEL POUSETTE-DART

This book is dedicated to four American artists
who consistently lived up to their highest
ambitions and ideals:
John Marin, Yasuo Kuniyoshi,
Bradley Walker Tomlin and Arshile Gorky.

LEE GATCH ***The Flame***

JOHN MARIN *Sunset*

For me painting is primarily a means of expression and a philosophy. I attempt to combine concept and formal structure into a unified whole. I do not believe the abstract and the real are in opposition, but rather are parts of an eternally interrelated whole that embraces all physical, mental and spiritual manifestations.

KENNETH CALLAHAN

MORRIS GRAVES ***Preening Sparrows***

EDWIN DICKINSON ***Ruin at Daphne***

I shall never forget or abandon the great and eternal canons of art for the bizarre, fragmentary, spectacular and fugitive — the fads. My adoration of the great ancients who exemplify the indestructible, immutable foundations of art for all time shall never dim nor tarnish. Their legacy has always been and will always be my spiritual refreshment and renewal. The great ancients worked with God. They interpreted and embodied the glory and wonder of space, of time, of the elements of humanity.

Impregnating the plastics with human passion, pathos, eloquence, spiritual aspiration and vision will put the artist on the way to the infinite, the universal and eternal. The artist who becomes entangled in the intellectual complexities and servile to the modern industrial gadgetry is building a scaffold but not an edifice . . . MAX WEBER

I usually develop a series of paintings at the same time, all of them concerned with a central idea. But this idea is only the initiating stimulus from the physical and emotional environment, no more than a point of departure. Many other things must go into the making of a picture; it is developed beyond the initiating stimulus until it leads an independent existence, becomes a new entity. BORIS MARGO

MITCHELL SIPORIN ***Aging Actress***

CARL G. NELSON *Maine Night No. 2*

GIORGIO CAVALLON

Abstract No. 6

HENRY McFEE ***Things on a Table***

I believe that professional art is never accidental or automatic but rather studied, planned and controlled with all of the knowledge and experience at the command of the individual. I want my work to be understood. Among the prerequisites inherent in the plastic arts are: devotion to craft, honor and humility to tradition, and a chosen area of reference. The depth of understanding demanded in fulfilling these prerequisites is an extended experience coming out of related reading, museums, stimulation from living practitioners and the sister arts. ROBERT GWATHMEY

BYRON BROWN ***Azoic Fugue***

It is not subject matter that differentiates one work from another, but feeling and form. It is never an original idea chiefly because there are no original ideas. The race is so old it is inconceivable that a newcomer can have a thought which has eluded our tragic and thoughtful species. That which puerile minds call original is usually only novel and often only bizarre. It is not the length but the depth of works that makes them great. The world is so much with us only intensity can penetrate and affect our over-frightened minds; and that intensity must have a form. Feeling and form are all; and that man is most an artist who fuses these two into an indivisible one.

TOM BENRIMO

JACK TWORKOV *Sirens in Voice*

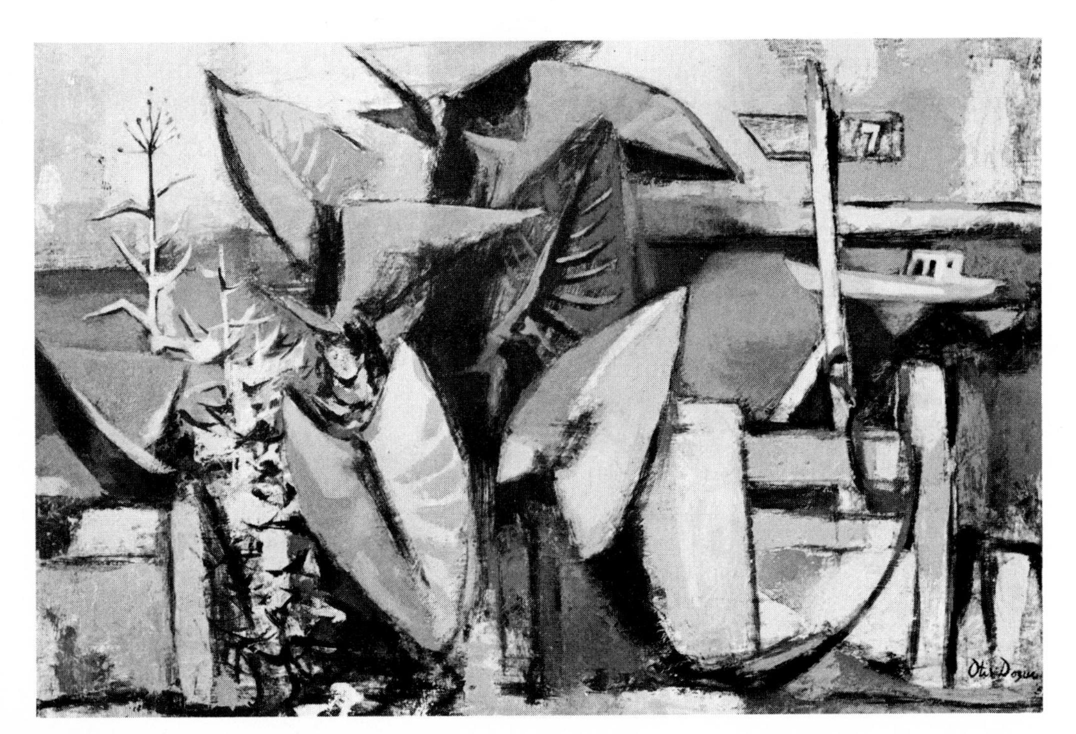

OTIS DOZIER

Passage to the Sea

I understand certain forms in spite of nature, and others because of nature; but it is always the amazement of existence which makes all my beginnings for me. The subject for me becomes not material which I simply pick or find, but something which emerges. The relationship between forms in space makes it emerge whenever I succeed in my work. . .

KURT FERDINAND ROESCH

SAMUEL M. ADLER ***Invocation***

SIGMUND MENKES

Boy Playing Harmonica

REUBEN TAM *Dark Wave*

XAVIER GONZALEZ *Landscape*

WILLIAM THON *Maine Granite Quarry*

GEORGE BEATTIE *Pisa*

I paint differently today than I did five years ago because I can express myself more clearly, but in a real sense I have not changed. I practice my art and pursue my ideal because of a strong conviction that I owe my being as a painter to our society. Regardless of the direction in which my work moves, I always attempt to reflect our time from its most humanistic point of view. In "Carnival" I portray the emotional duplicity of our period. In a world of festive "deadpan" the grimness of the reality is heightened by the color of unreality.

YASUO KUNIYOSHI

LEONID *Provincetown*

My humble wish is to always have the time to paint, the materials with which to paint, and something to say in paint. SEYMOUR FOGEL

CHARLES OSCAR *Night Journey*

CHARLES SHEELER ***Manchester***

The contemporary artist working in a non-objective idiom is interested in something that goes beyond mere structure, composition and plastic unity. He may be searching for forms that will have for him and for his audience the magic symbolic meaning that exists in the work of primitive and religious art. Our tragedy is to live in a time that has no organized iconography, no religion, no symbols for worship or ritual, as was the case in Egypt, Greece, earlier Christianity and in primitive societies. ERLE LORAN

JOHN VON WICHT ***Harbor Festivity***

The artist's interest in art is not separable from his concern with the whole world of idea and of effort. Intellectual, emotional, moralistic, revolutionary towards everything in life — limited only by his energy, of which the artist must be generously possessed. BALCOMB GREENE

PAUL MOMMER ***Studio Interior No. 2***

No man has ever done anything creatively worthwhile without the capacity to love. No artist can create without it. It is his whole motivation, and as such the love comes first, not the artist . . . Man is not big enough to go it alone. To attempt to do so he must kill love, the very thing and the only thing that can bring him to fulfillment. By the blind determination to create, he kills creation. Creation belongs to the warm heart with a capacity for contentment and in acknowledgment of the irrevocable laws of nature.

LOUIS BOUCHE

GEORGE PICKEN *East River Rooftops*

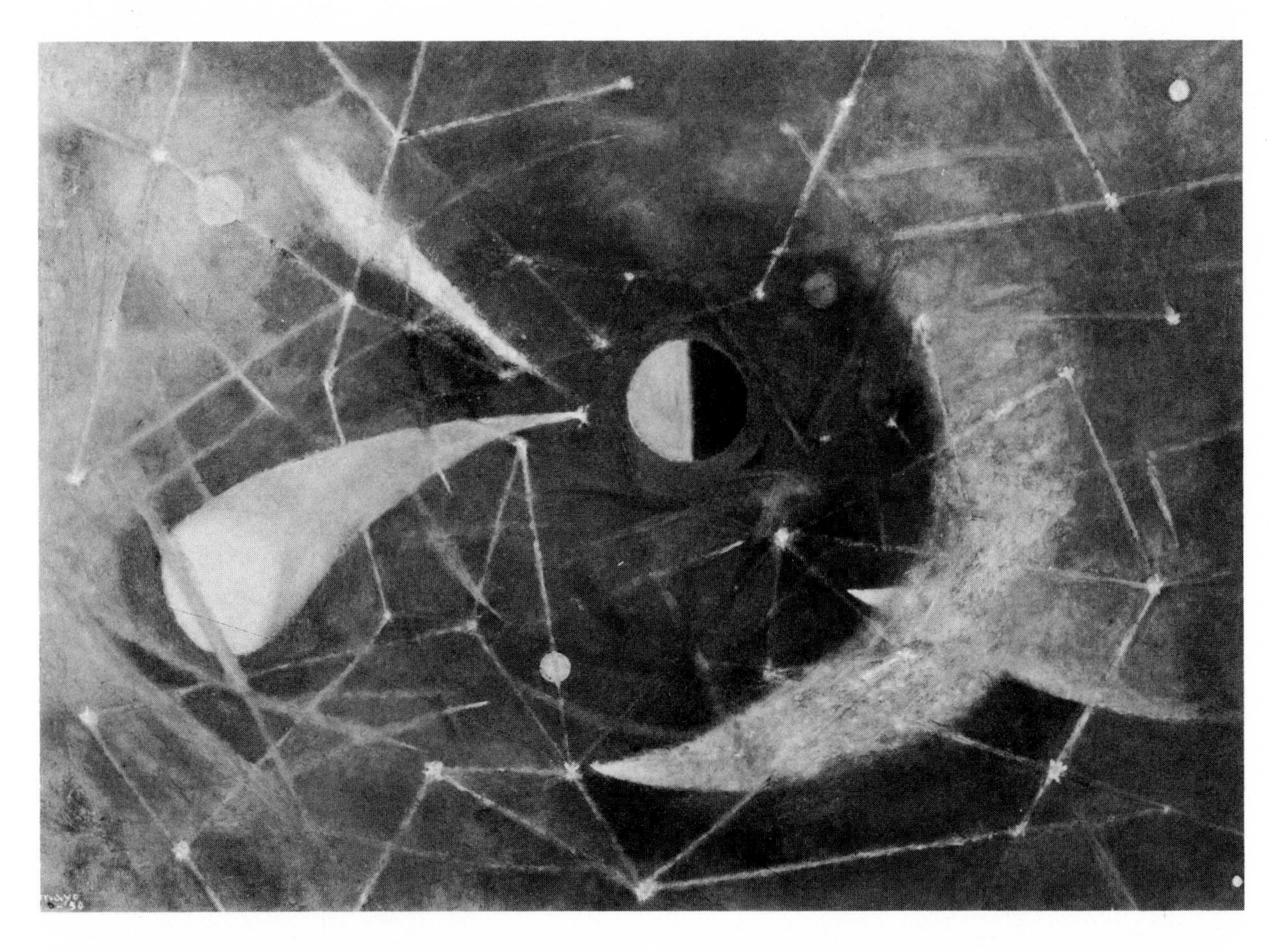

RUFINO TAMAYO ***The Heavens***

Art is the articulation of man's intellectual, spiritual, emotional and aesthetic impulses in relation to life, as experience. I paint not what I see, but what I feel, not what I think, but rather what I am. It is not for art to hold a mirror to nature (to freeze a moment out of time) but rather to capture an impulse and sustain it into all eternity.

The dimension that lies beyond the measurable pictorial, is perhaps the all important one. There is for me, a "magic" in art, a strange, deeply moving force which makes itself felt but cannot be analyzed. It is in Beethoven and Brahms, in El Greco and Rembrandt – and in the great cathedrals of Europe. I do believe, that in the final analysis, it is this dimension that constitutes for us our criterion of judgment. SAMUEL M. ADLER

ARSHILE GORKY *The Betrothal II*

THE ARTIST AS CRITIC

"In all media, the death of Art is to please all and offend none."
Marya Mannes, in *Reporter* Magazine.

THE CONTEMPORARY art of our time is not so revolutionary as it seems — rather it is evolutionary in its growth and development. Art over the centuries has developed in great spirals. A spiral begins under the impetus of a primitive feeling for expression; then slowly emerges into realism. From realism it is a natural transition to expressionism. Then it matures and passes into abstractionism, and eventually returns to primitivism again.

Before the advent of modern science and technology the arts underwent a slow development within each culture; but today, because of the tremendous advances in transportation and communication, they have taken on an international character. At present we are in a transient period of non-representationalism where experimentation plays an important role. This may lead to either good or bad results, depending on whether or not the artist is concerned primarily with cleverness and publicity or with a genuine desire to broaden the field of aesthetic expression. There are signs of attempts by individuals and groups to solidify so-called modern expression into set formulas and techniques. This can result only in stylization; and when stylization sets in, painting is on the road to decadence. However, there are the makings of a great renaissance of art in this country if its inspired creative artists live up to their highest ideals, have the courage of their inmost convictions, and retain their basic sincerity.

The vital artist responds only to those things which deeply move and inspire him. He does not arbitrarily limit himself to the life and art of one period; he instinctively feels that all the world is his hunting ground — the world of yesterday, today and tomorrow. When he borrows something from a bygone civilization, he recreates it in the crucible of his emotion and imagination so that it emerges as something new, with a life of its own.

Creative artists are always modern. They live intensely within their time. They are conscious of their environment, but they do not allow the tawdry, superficial aspects of it to dominate their work. The sincere artist has the courage of his own convictions. He accepts mutability but refuses to be overwhelmed by it; he lives intensely in the present moment but realizes its relationship to the past and to the future. He is not dominated by fads and fashions but searches always for the powerful aesthetic expression of a timeless truth.

In art circles today one subject is endlessly discussed. "Should art be realistic or abstract?" Actually all the great significant art of the world contains both realism and abstraction. James Johnson Sweeney has clearly expressed his opinion on this subject, ". . .painting is not a pure art, no form, or element of form in the painter's repertory is without roots in some combination of physical experiences from the world of nature. As a consequence no pictorial form can exist deprived of association of one sort or other, both for the artist and the observer." Even Mondrian, who carried abstraction to a hitherto undreamed of extreme, admitted that his original conception of a simple criss-cross construction came from the sight of a building that was being torn down.

If Mr. Sweeney is right there is no such thing as pure, non-objective art. When painting tries to free itself entirely from nature, it becomes mere stylized decoration.

It is not uncommon to hear expressed the idea that basically all the arts are alike. It is true that all the arts have certain fundamental principles in common. Their differences arise from the fact that they serve different ends, and that these ends determine their own means.

The painter has one main objective: the expression of powerfully-felt concepts. The architect is concerned with function; for his object is to furnish living and working quarters for his clients. An illustrator must use his best energies towards the interpretation and visualization of an author's concept; while the advertising artist and the designer are concerned with the selling of merchandise or of ideas. Within the limitations of his own field each artist may create distinguished and significant work. Herbert Read has said, "What men do makes them what they are: *how* they do what they do determines the *quality* of what they are: and it is only when the doing is raised to the dignity of a regular or ritualistic art that it penetrates into the deepest recesses of the soul."

Every artist expresses what he is in every line, tone, texture, color and form he puts on his canvas. It is possible to discover his basic character traits and his abilities from his brush strokes, in much the same way as does a graphologist from his handwriting.

The artist in making a painting gives it a definite character. Over the years the painting itself does not change, except as time affects it. What does change is the attitude towards it of the public. This attitude is strongly influenced by the opinions of critics, and the fashions and styles of the moment. The intelligent critic is one who sensitively, intelligently and imaginatively appraises the work for its own creative value and who, in making such an appraisal, is not influenced by the vogue of any given period. The second-rate critic tries to tell the artist wherein his work is lacking without first fully comprehending what he is trying to express. Reliable criticism can come only from direct contact with works of art over the years. Thomas Munro has said that there is still a wide gulf between aestheticians and creative artists, and that often students taking college courses in aesthetics discover, on graduation, that they know very little about actual creative works of art. In 1928 Thomas Munro wrote a book entitled *Scientific Method in Aesthetics,* from which the following is quoted: "Perhaps, as often charged, our whole system of education in the arts, especially in colleges, is such as to make critics rather than artists. Perhaps education can have little effect one way or other, and the appearance of creativeness will always be an unpredictable, uncontrollable miracle."

Unquestionably scientific methods may be applied to better modes of comprehending and evaluating art, but when such methods are applied to creation itself they become destructive. Examples of such so-called scientific methods are the Hambidge theory of Dynamic Symmetry and the Schillinger method of manufacturing music. "Art" produced by the application of such methods is vapid, mechanical and uncreative. It might be well for artists to make a concerted effort to formulate their own ideas as to how and in what directions art should develop, instead of leaving these vital questions to critics and aestheticians.

One of the elements in painting of which artists are now aware is that of chance. Chance as used in art is not the same as accident. Chance, to be creatively potent, must spring from the subconscious. It has nothing in common with trickiness or superficial cleverness. Clever and tricky design has a legitimate use in selling merchandise, because this field is dominated by fashion and by the demands of the moment. Only after a creative painting has been made, may it legitimately be used in a functional way, either on the wall of a room or as an illustration for a magazine article or an advertisement.

There is a good deal of difference between the work of an amateur and that of a mature creative artist. Aestheticians and instructors should make clear the difference between these two types of expression. One has the primitive charm inherent in the untutored expression of a child; the other requires experience, creative power and organization which can come only from maturity. No mature person can paint like a child, however much he may try. A few self-taught artists like Rousseau, Bombois, Bauchant and John Kane have a naturally primitive and child-like approach to their work, because their innate creative qualities were not destroyed by wrong methods of teaching.

No work which does not start with an inspired conception of over-all unity can be truly creative. The Gestalt Theory that the whole creates its parts is demonstrably true, although it is equally true that every part must have a significance of its own. This significance, however, must emerge from its relationship to the original conception. An inspiration mght be defined as the instantaneous realization of a unified living whole. However it often happens that an artist after starting a painting will have a second, third or even a fourth inspiration while working on a canvas. But every time this happens he must create a totally new work. Matisse and Picasso have often demonstrated that it is possible to create a number of different paintings by using the same initial subject matter.

An inspiration may be preceded by research and intellectual preoccupation with certain materials, but the inspiration itself can never be intellectually and consciously induced. Benedetto Croce states this idea succinctly, "Art is imagination or intuition, the first primitive stage of the spirit, sharply differentiated from knowledge obtained through the intellect."

The creative idea for a work of art might be likened to a seed. Within the seed are all the potential ingredients for the making of a rose, a stalk of wheat or an oak tree. In other words, living works of art cannot be thought out, planned or organized until after they have been inspirationally visioned.

Nowadays the word "functional" is sometimes used as though it meant the same thing as the word "creative." Function in itself has never created a work of art. A work of art can be created only by an artist. When an African hunter fashions a shield as a protection against the attacks of wild beasts, it is a work of art not because of its function, but because the man who made it was an artist.

Henry Russel Hitchcock says, in *Painting Toward Architectur*e, "Architecture inevitably exists through time, not merely as the momentary structural solution of a closed functional equation." Some examples of our modern architecture might be critized on the ground that although they are functionally successful they are not works of art. This is because they possess neither outward nor inward *living* quality.

Some paintings fail because they have not been carried to completion, because they are labored, because they have been carried too far. Paul Klee says, "To know when to stop is of the same importance as to know when to begin. To continue automatically is as much a sin against the creative spirit as to start work without a true inspiration."

To comprehend and to enjoy a creative work of art, orientation and effort are needed. Although the essence of a painting may be felt and understood quickly, it requires concentration and study to fully grasp the sum total of its unification and the organization of all of its constant aesthetic qualities.

NATHANIEL POUSETTE-DART

YASUO KUNIYOSHI *Amazing Juggler*

RICO LEBRUN *Rooster on the Arm of the Cross*

The lithograph, *Abstract No. 1* by Louis Shanker, reproduced in color facing page 82, was selected because it has the plastic qualities we associate with painting. During the last fifty years the cleavage between the different technical media of expression has largely disappeared. A painting today may be made up of various materials and may use several different art media.

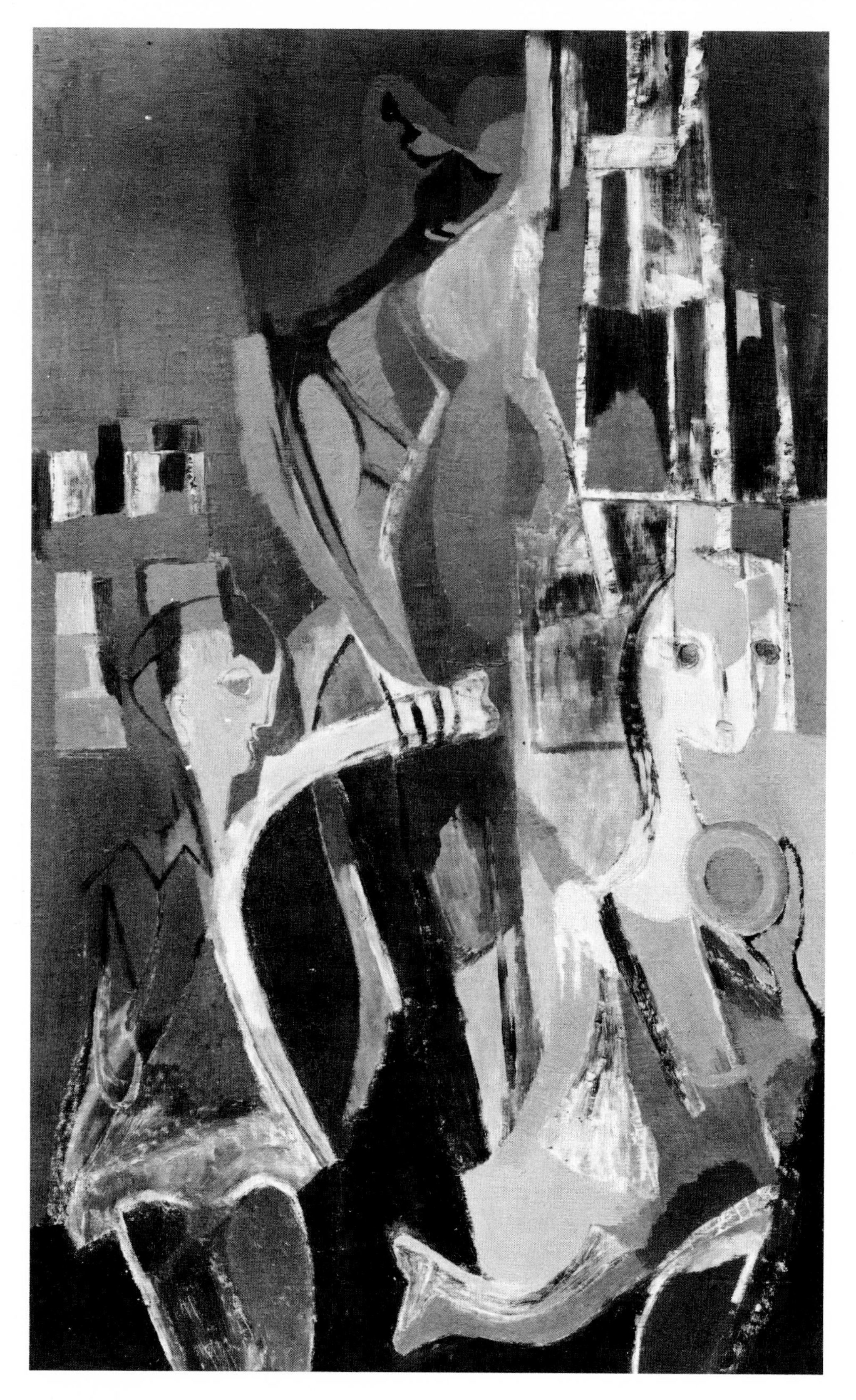

KURT ROESCH *Walk in Town*

NATHANIEL POUSETTE-DART ***Renaissance***

I do not believe there is such a thing as non-objective art. All the forms one sees in a painting or piece of sculpture, all the colors, textures and combinations of such are to be found in nature. One has only to look far enough to see that they exist. Let us concern ourselves about good and bad art, and not fret about silly categories. BYRON BROWNE

Art is intuitive, and not related to the scientific discoveries – such as the knowledge of anatomy, the laws of perspective, and the systems and harmonies of color harmony based on the spectrum, These have had their influence on the outward forms of expression, but did not and could not add anything to the basic nature of art itself – which is a reflection of man's intuitive reaction to his environment or his speculation concerning the world of which he is part. Reality in art is not confined to any particular form of expression. PAUL MOMMER

HOWARD COOK *The Bridge No. 1*

MARGARET PETERSON *Man's Child*

CHARLES BIRCHFIELD *Sun and Rocks*

I believe that painting, whether representational or non-representational, must speak through the picture elements themselves. First of all one must really believe those elements have meaning in relation to nature and man's experiences, emotional and intellectual. To me the physical laws constitute the greatest bond in good painting of all times. CARL NELSON

BROR UTTER *Pharmaceutic Cabinet*

JOSEPH ALBERS ***Homage to the Square***

My philosophy is the reality of space and light; an ever-flowing, never-ceasing continuity; unfettered by man-made machinery, weight and external likenesses. I use geometric symbols as they represent structural essences and contain infinite possibilities of change and dynamics.

I. RICE PEREIRA

BENJAMIN WIGFALL ***Chimneys***

JOHN SENNHAUSER *Synchroformic 27*

VIKTOR SCHRECKENGOST *Fish Forms*

IVAN ALBRIGHT ***The Wild Bunch***

Line, Texture, Form and Space employed for their own sake on a wall or canvas are capable of entertaining, but many artists in the past made good paintings using the form of human beings and natural objects in pictures which also entertain. Use of the same or similar material now or tomorrow does not necessarily make the work or the author of it obsolete. This material is timeless and interesting to people of all epochs if seen through new eyes and set down in original and freshly created ways. The sweet, the heroic, the tender, the sad and the humorous are in people who walked in the past and in the present worlds. People today have the same virtues, failings, perfections and distortions that they had in Memling's or Giotto's time.

PHILIP EVERGOOD

I believe the creative act is the extraordinary change from the perception of a visual reality to the effective projection of the visual image. A radar distortion resulting from an intellectual-emotional-physical awareness to the many aspects of reality.

KEITH FINCH

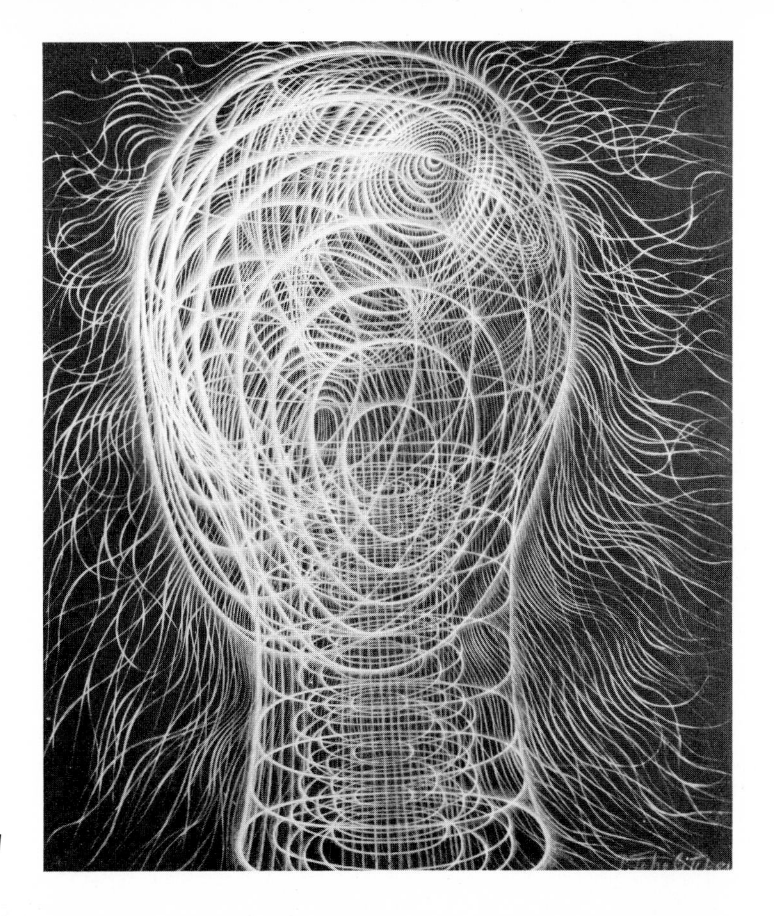

PAVEL TCHELITCHEW *Revolving Head*

MARK TOBEY *Orpheus*

CHARLES GRIFFEN FARR ***A Street in Knoxville***

I try to intensify and condense.
I want my painting to say all I think, or know, or feel about a given subject.
I do not think literal representation will say enough.
A subject handled as a total abstraction seldom says all that I want it to say.

OTIS DOZIER

In our time the painter has two sources: Nature and Art. Both must be transformed to produce a work of art. BROR UTTER

DEAN ELLIS *Scrap*

CHARLES SHAW *Tonal Rhapsody*

JOHN ANDERSON *Creation of Eve*

WILLIAM BRICE *Rose Sequence*

MORRIS KANTOR *The Summertime*

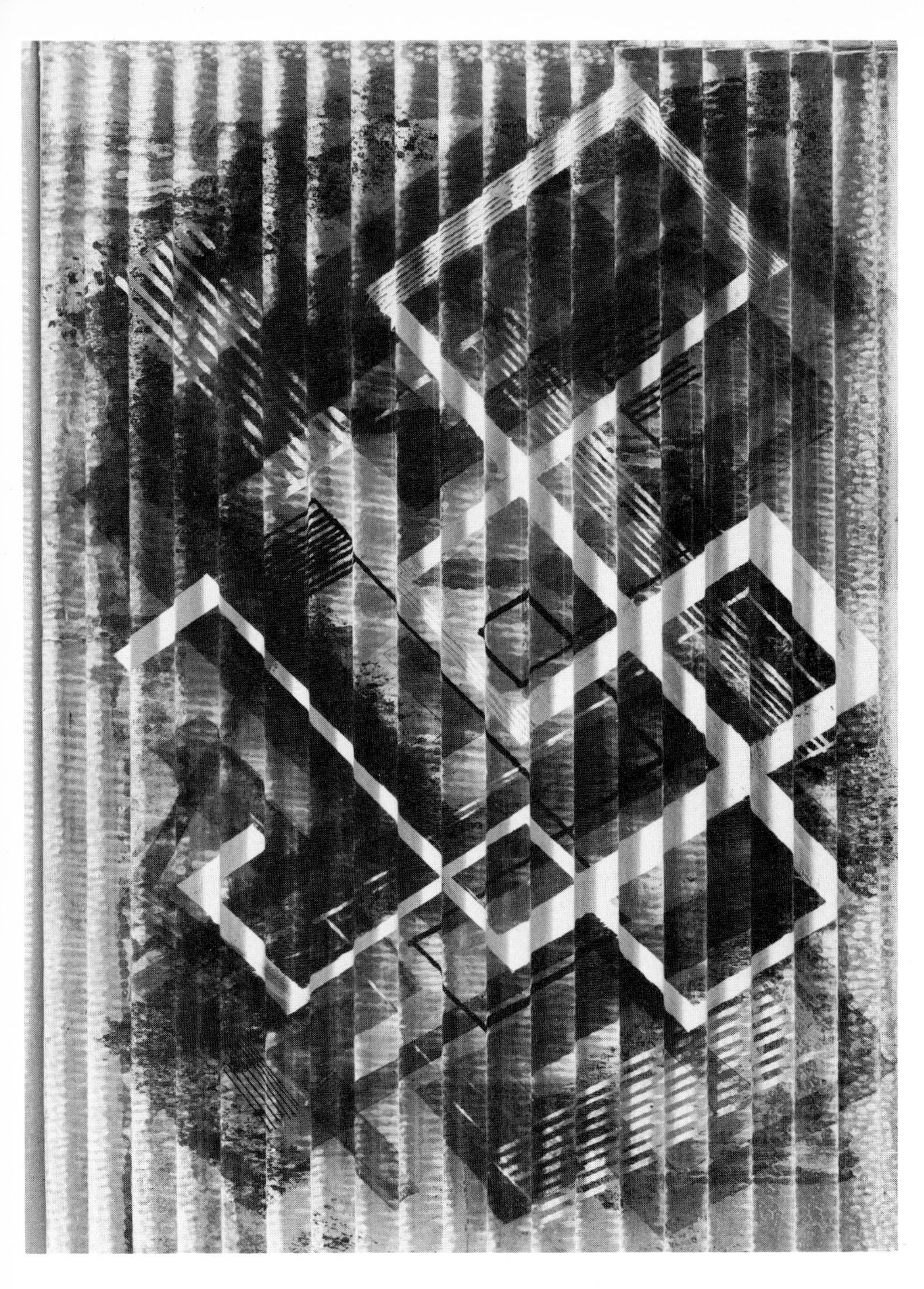

I. RICE PEREIRA *Ruby Flux*

. . . Truly the eye was not made to take inventory like an auctioneer, nor to flirt with delusions and recognitions like a maniac. It was made to cast a lineament, a conducting wire between the most heterogeneous things.
ANDRE BRETON

From the catalogue of a Gorky exhibition, Julian Levy Gallery.

WILLIAM De KOONING ***Excavation***

I strive to satisfy my soul through expression, making structures which have significance and beauty as things within themselves — a life which goes onward and onward in its feeling — its joy of being — its desire to interpenetrate and mingle and be a part of all other life.

RICHARD POUSETTE-DART

John Marin, in his studio, critically examining his work. Photo. by George Daniell.

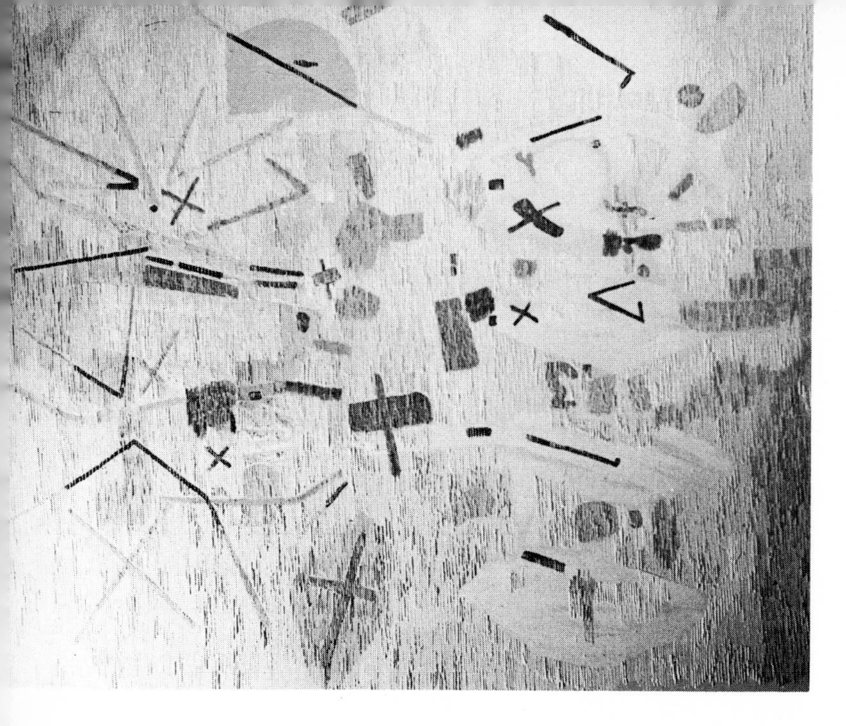

LEE MULLICAN ***Salt Fire***

Ours is a universal time and the significances of such a time all point to the need for the universalizing of the consciousness and the conscience of man. It is in the awareness of this that our future depends unless we are to sink into a universal dark age.

MARK TOBEY

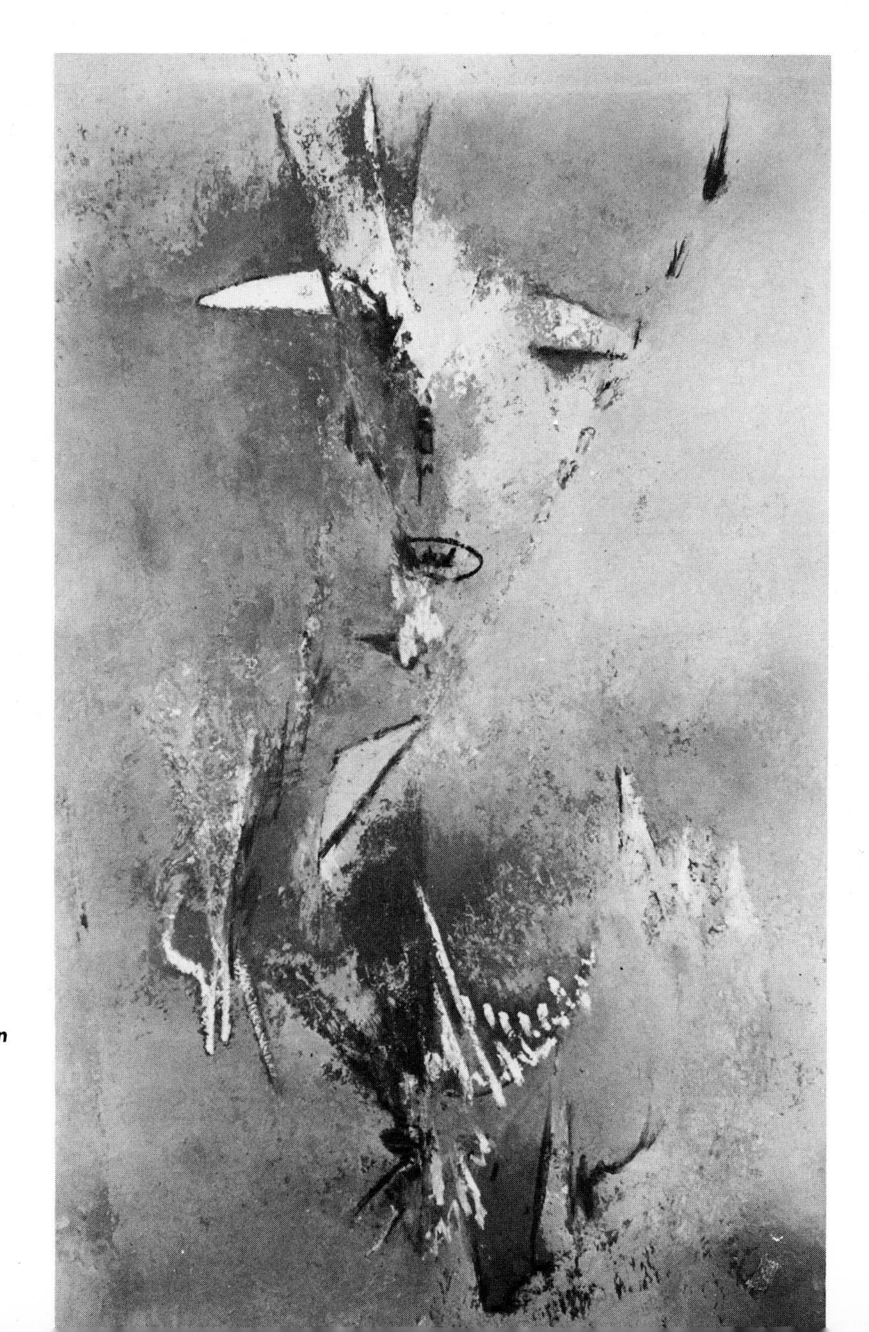

MAUD MORGAN ***Descension***

RICHARD POUSETTE-DART *The Magnificent*

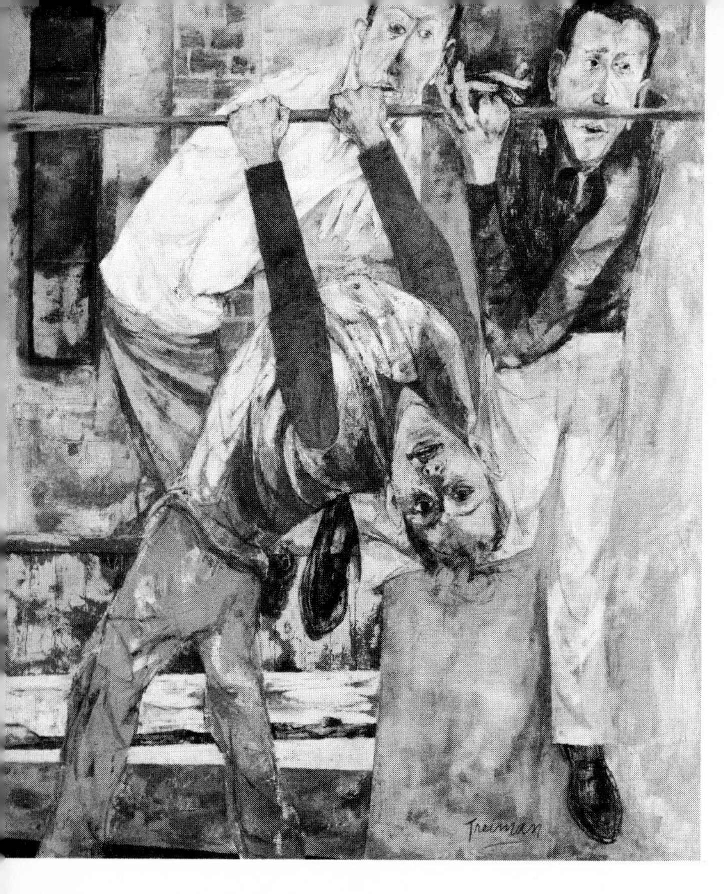

JOYCE TREIMAN ***Escape***

I am excited by and interested in new media, for I live in an age of change. Yet I guard this enthusiasm, so that I shall not be merely in fashion or involved in a senseless mania for novelty and innovation. SYD SOLOMON

SIEGFRIED REINHARDT ***Sentinel***

HELEN LUNDEBERG ***The Mirror***

For me, painting is a slow crystalization of an idea — a development of the idea into design, form and color. I have chosen for subject, man, his relationship to the world.

GEORGE TOOKER

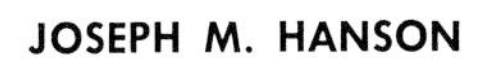

JOSEPH M. HANSON ***Composition***

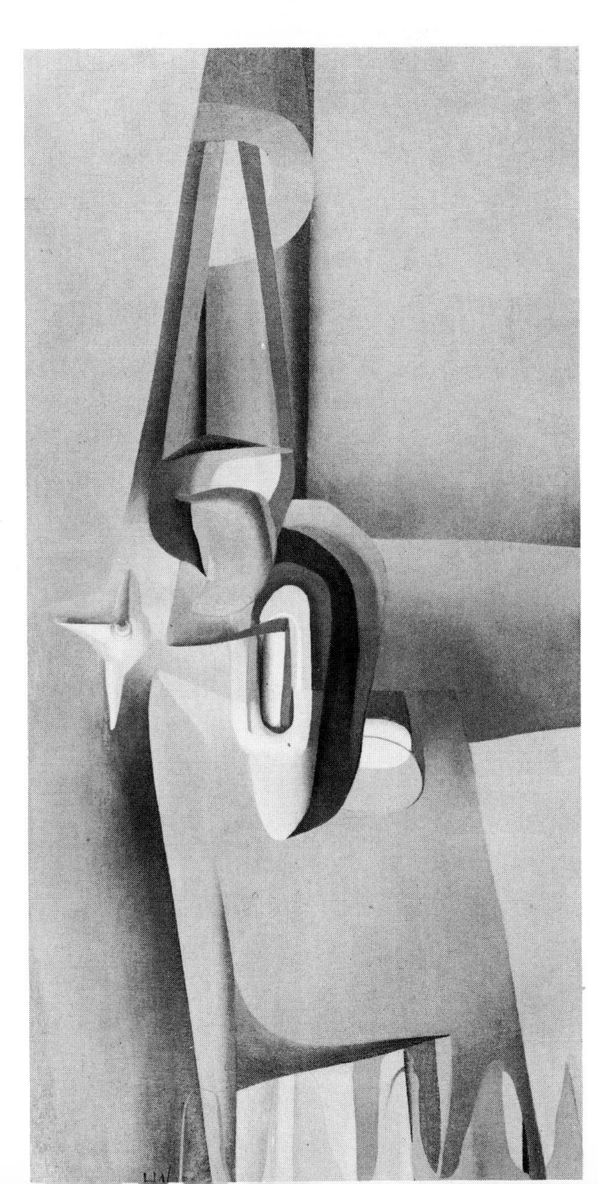

KARL ZERBE *Apartment No. 2*

I struggle to achieve meaning and insight rather than surface pyrotechnics for their own sake. My subject matter is myself, the medium through which life as I understand it, assumes form and content.

SIEGFRIED REINHARDT

JOHN SLOAN *Riders in the Hills*

ABRAHAM RATTNER ***Farm Composition No. 1***

I revere everything in nature that I paint but my fidelity is not to it but to the canvas in front of me. My painting can be called representational to the extent that it might help a person looking at the actual scene or a photograph of it to see more interest there. For the rest, I simply try to be painterly.

MARNYE REINHART

RICHARD SEARS ***Towards Integrating Sculptural Influences***

I believe that art is the child of nature. When I paint I work usually directly from nature and contrary to critics, I am not rediscovering nature, because I never left it. My abstract idiom is a point of departure for the expression and in line with the grand painters of the Hudson River school. In other words I believe that all the good painting in the United States has its roots in nature and is abstracted. THEODOROS STAMOS

I believe that the outer reality must be studied in order to arrive finally at the inner reality. The movement of forms, the sense of scale, the feeling of being both inside and outside the tree, were important aspects for me in this picture.

WILLIAM KIENBUSCH

EDWARD D. LEWANDOWSKI

Gulf Coast Shipyard

FRANK DUNCAN ***Within Autumn***

JOHN HELIKER *Palazzo*

I paint to rest from the phenomena of the external world – to pronounce and to make notations of its essences with which to verify the inner eye.

MORRIS GRAVES

I believe it is necessary to accept the limitations of the painter's means, to know them well and to make them one's own. Personal expression, uncontrolled, is a silly thing. I do not underestimate the value of the accidental and emotional approach. I cultivate it. It is a valuable part of intuition, new ventures, new visions, new possibilities, drama and shock. However before these can be full expressions they must be given power through the laws of composition (structure, balance, unity, etc.). Only then is the intent of artist revealed.

CAMERON BOOTH

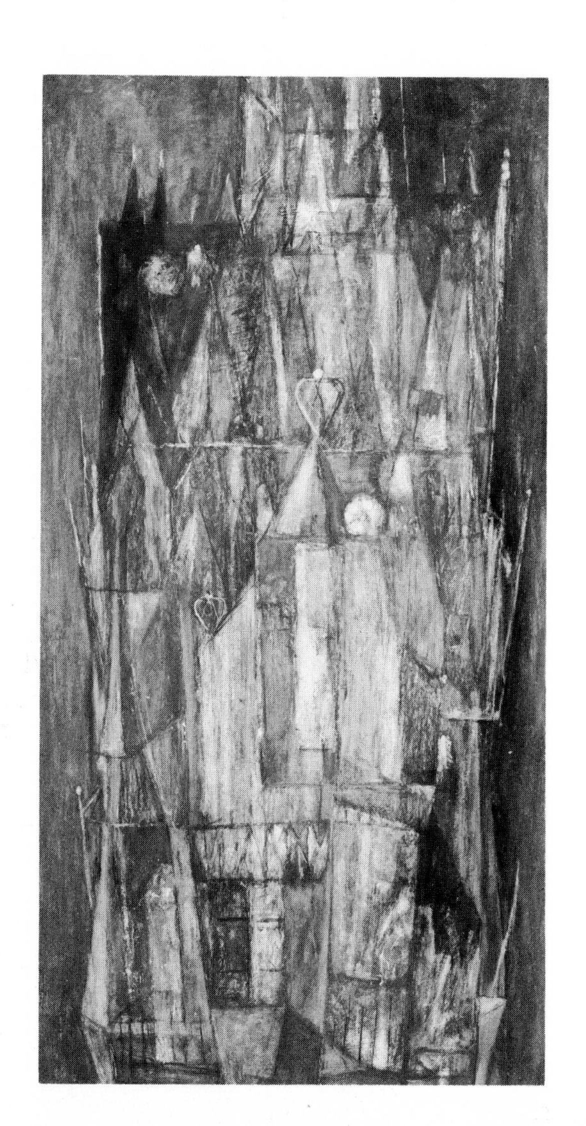

JOSEPH FRIEBERT *Synagogue*

CARLYLE BROWNE *Table with Glasses and Roses*

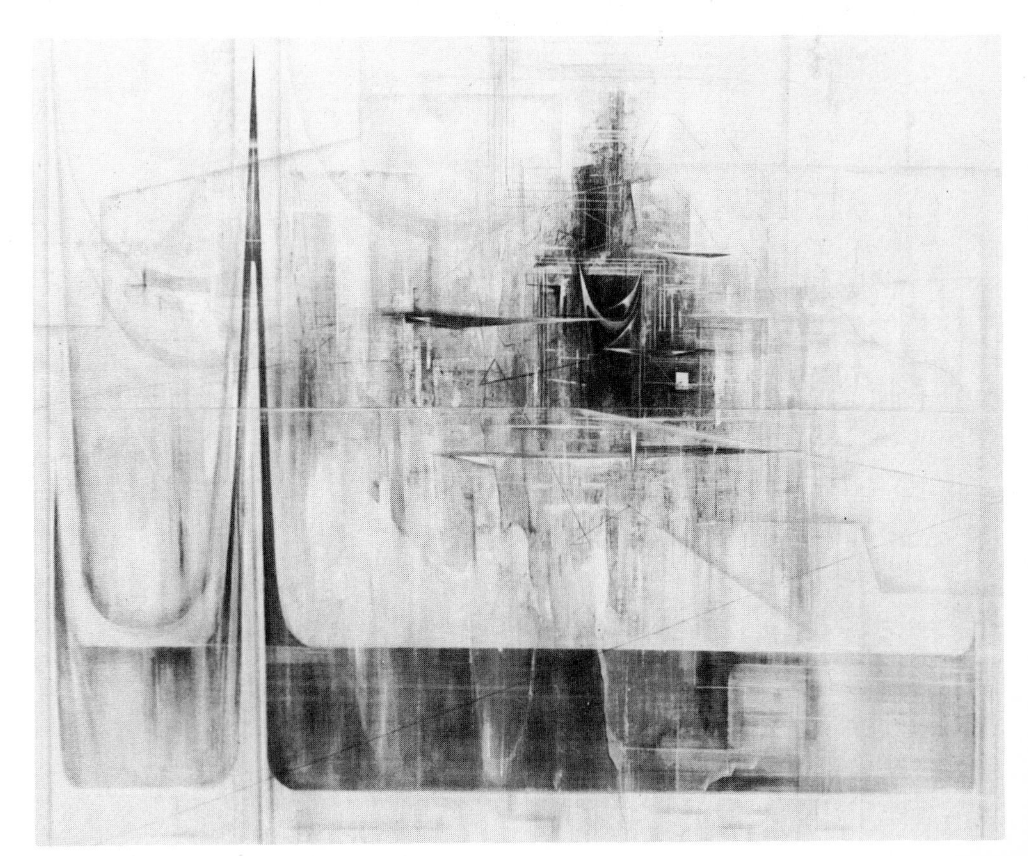

TOM BENRIMO
Reflections

JACKSON POLLOCK *No. 12*

When J. S. Bach plays the organ, God goes to the Mass. AMEDEE J. OZENFANT

ADOLF DEHN *Haitian Heaven*

A painting is its own comment. Its only interpretation is told by the eye. It is enough to look, see and gain pleasure by that sense. The painter has put everything there, the spectator takes away what he wishes or what he sees.

CARLYLE BROWN

JAMES BROOK *No. 44*

KAHLIL GIBRAN *The China Shop*

My wish is to make something permanent out of the transitory, by means at once dramatic and colloquial. Certain moments have the gift of revealing the past and foretelling the future. It is these moments that I hope to catch. LOREN MAC IVER

HERBERT KATZMAN *Two Nudes before Japanese Screen*

ADOLPH GOTTLIEB ***The Frozen Sounds***

HANS HOFMAN ***Blue Enchantment***

STUART DAVIS *Tournos*

PETER BLUME *Crucifixion*

In the Arts of the past, the integration of the plastic Arts was accomplished by addition (frescoes, bas-relief). The Art of today has accomplished integration by synthesis. Relational Painting – A Step by Step Development Toward the Essential Integration of All Plastic Art.

FRITZ GLARNER

ALEANDER BROOK ***Remnants***

There are two ways in which I develop a painting. Many times I begin without a preconceived idea, making use of the artistic elements of line, color and form, which approach tends to create a solely abstract configuration. As I work along in this manner I discover within the form an associative implication which I try to clarify and organize without destroying the original abstract idea. At other times I start with a pre-designated concept of subject matter and then try to work the design factor around this associative form. Whichever of the two methods is employed and however important the abstract content, a personal relationship with nature ultimately tends to manifest itself, each force contributing to the definition of the other. JOSEPH FRIEBERT

I have always painted figuratively because it is the only method adequate for my purpose; because the associations, the "meanings" of recognizable forms are necessary to the kind of poetic entities I wish to create.

HELEN LUNDEBERG

WALTER MURCH ***Blocks***

I hope to make my paintings simple enough to directly touch all those who want to look. This seems to me more likely through non-representational work . . . MAUD MORGAN

LEWIS BUCK ***Iotrio***

WILLIAM KIENBUSCH *Twin Pine*

KARL KNATHS *Red Clock*

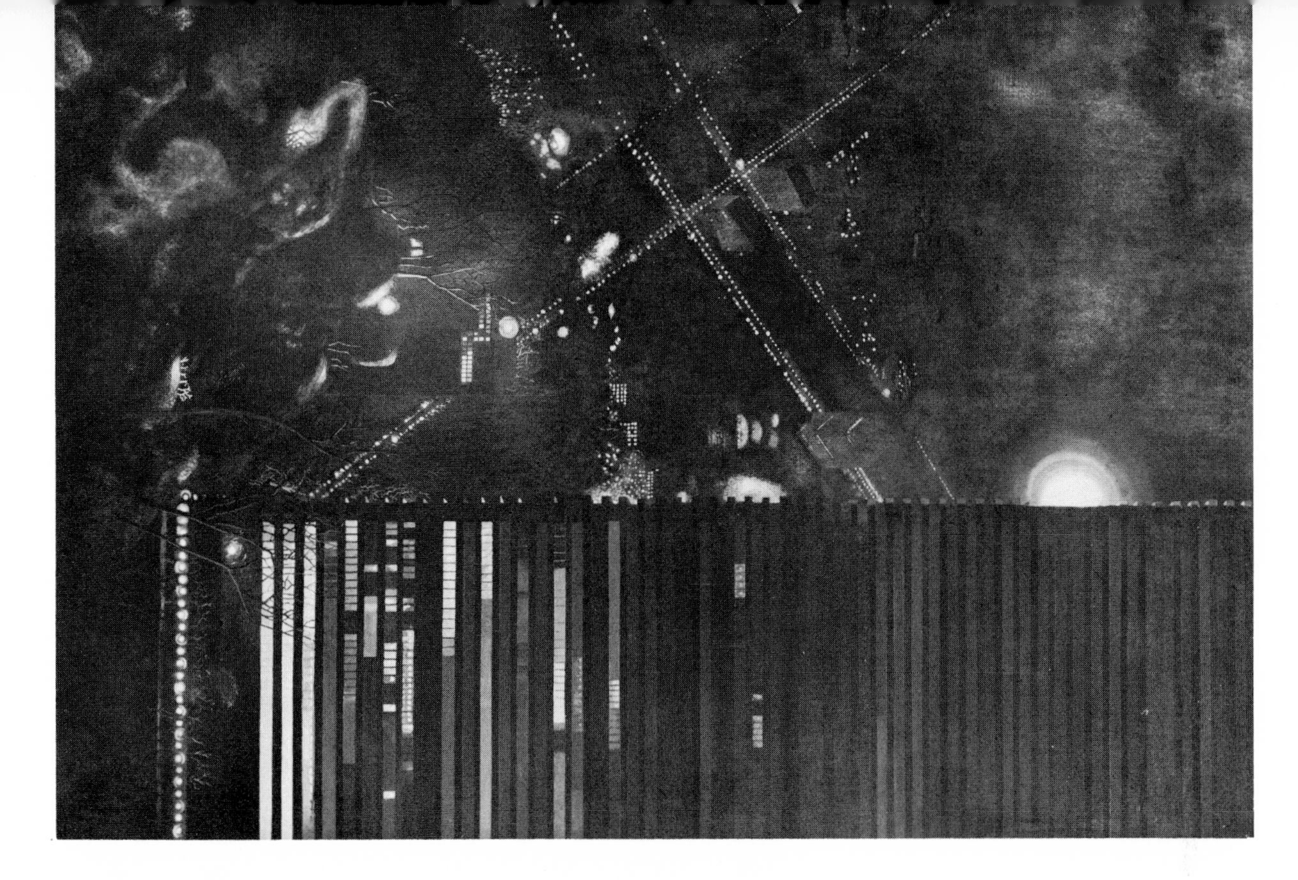

AMÉDEÉ J. OZENFANT

Building in a Park

WILLIAM M. HALSEY

The Onlookers

EDWARD JOHN STEVENS, JR. *The Red Bird*

The problem in painting, art, the world, would seem to be the balancing and intergrating of opposed forces. In these terms, if I have a credo, it would be:
Don't bluff.
Don't show off.
Try to use all that I know.
To learn more.
Do the best job that I can.

RICHARD L. SEARS

JOHN ATHERTON *Rocky Farmyard*

BRIAN CONNELLY *Attraction*

DUNCAN R. STUART *Matrix*

Today there are many new ways to live and feel and paint. Non-objective painting calls for tremendous flexibility and character on the part of the artist. The past exists today only as we understand it and discard it and symbols from the past, therefore, become meaningless. Painters must go ahead forging new paths as they have always; or art cannot breathe, and will not live. FELIX RUVOLO

THEODOROS STAMOS *Death of the Anarchist*

MARNYE REINHARDT *View Into Maryland*

JACK LEVINE *Under the El*

CAMERON BOOTH *Evening*

HENRY MATTSON ***Headland***

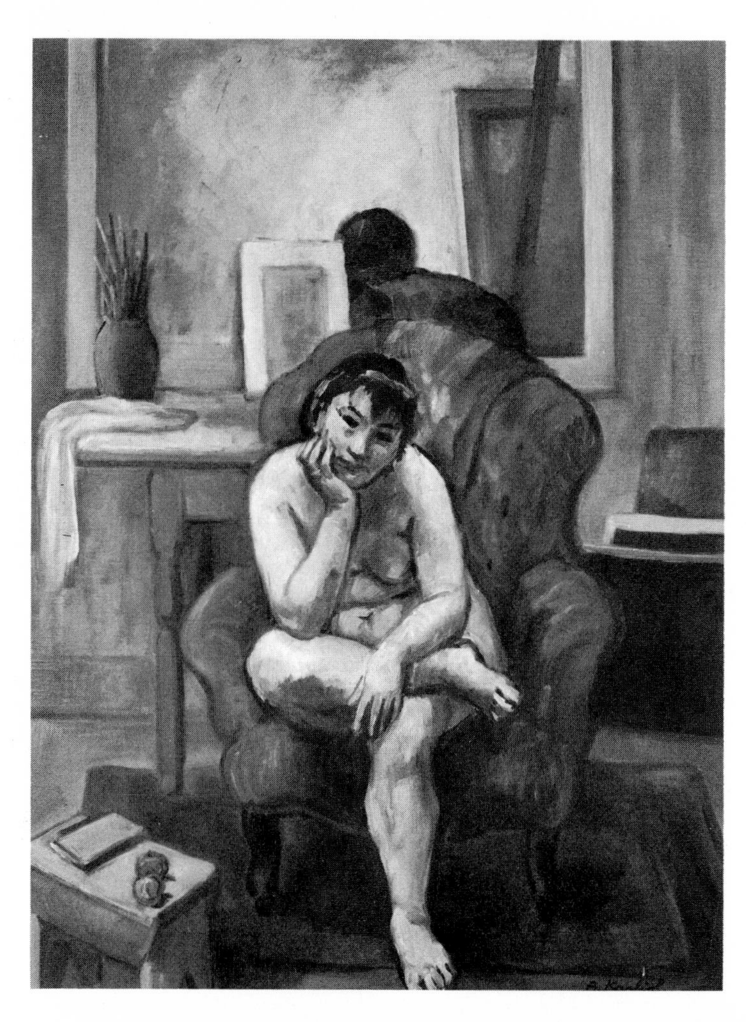

. . . intellectually I have yet to see a work of art that is purely emotional. Emotionally I have yet to see a work of art that is purely intellectual.

JOHN SENNHAUSER

BERNARD KARFIOL ***Repose***

WILLIAM LESTER *Old Fort Davis, Two Story*

GEORGE TOOKER *The Subway*

LOUIS BOUCHE *High Street Bus Barn*

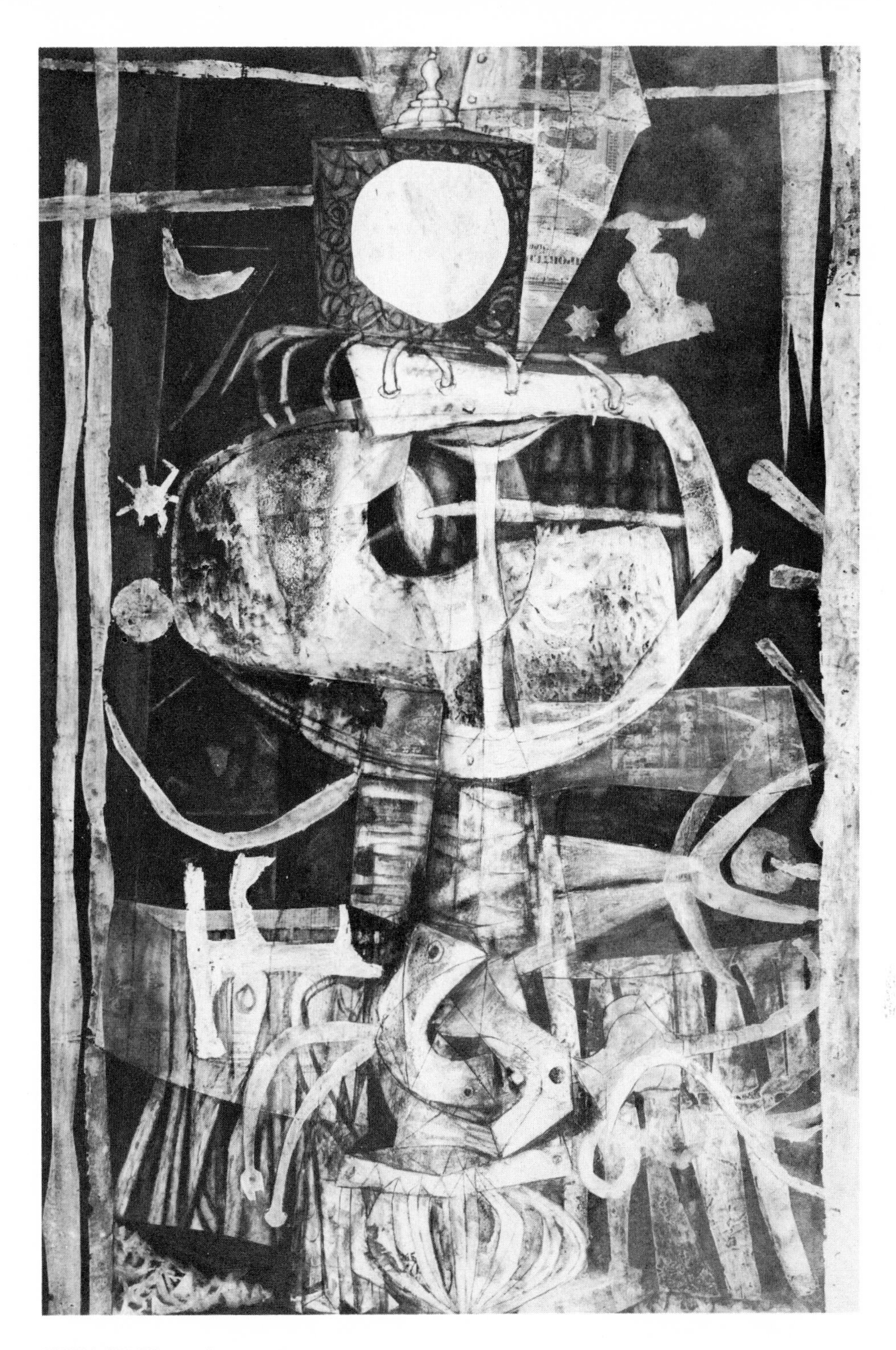

KEITH FINCH ***Locomotive***

. . . In dealing with ideas, vision and techniques for the task of communicating to the many, I hope for the day when a few of us, by using contemporary techniques (the camera, animation, the hand-made montage), will finally correlate some of the facts of contemporary vision, and collectively, even unanimously, say what we feel about the world around us.

RICO LEBRUN

CARL GAERTNER ***Bend in Storm King***

CARL MORRIS

Riders No. 10

LOUIS SHANKER

Abstract No. 1

VACLAV VYTLACIL ***Images of Pompeii***

A painter is like an orator who avoids rhetorical tricks and cliches, and whose words always give the impression of being the well-clad, faithful servants of his thought. KURT SELIGMANN

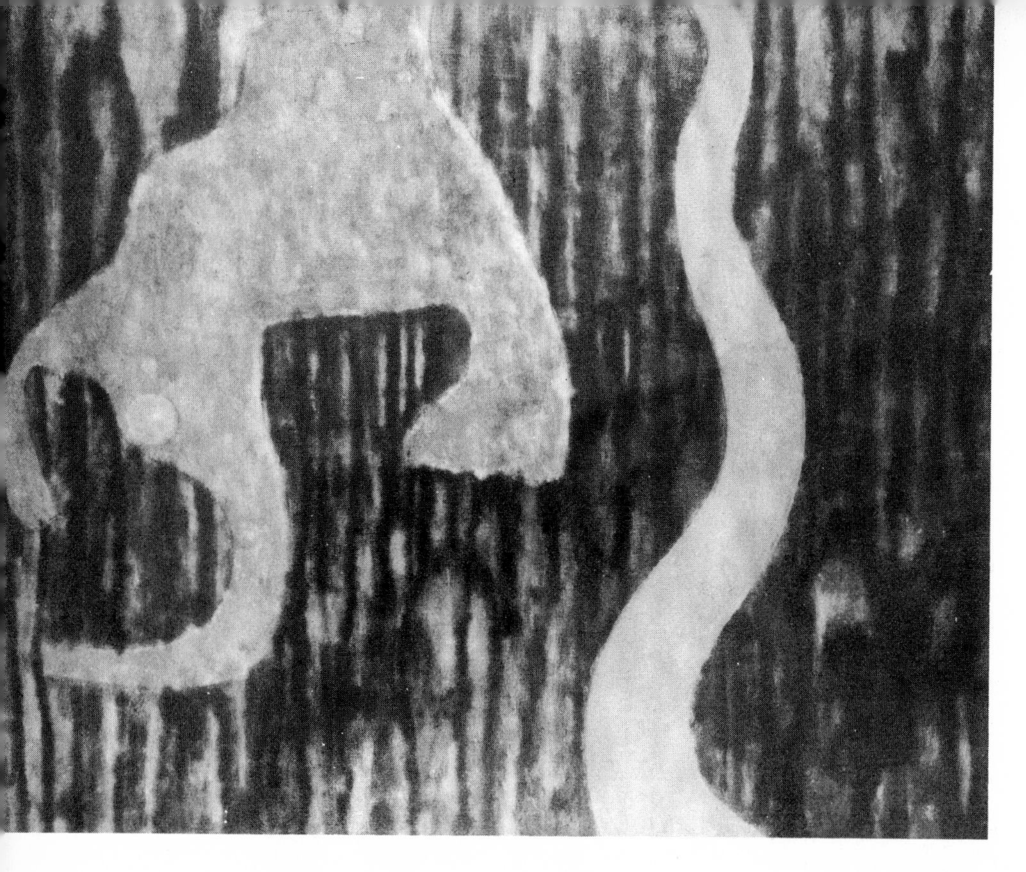

WILLIAM BAZIOTES *Jungle*

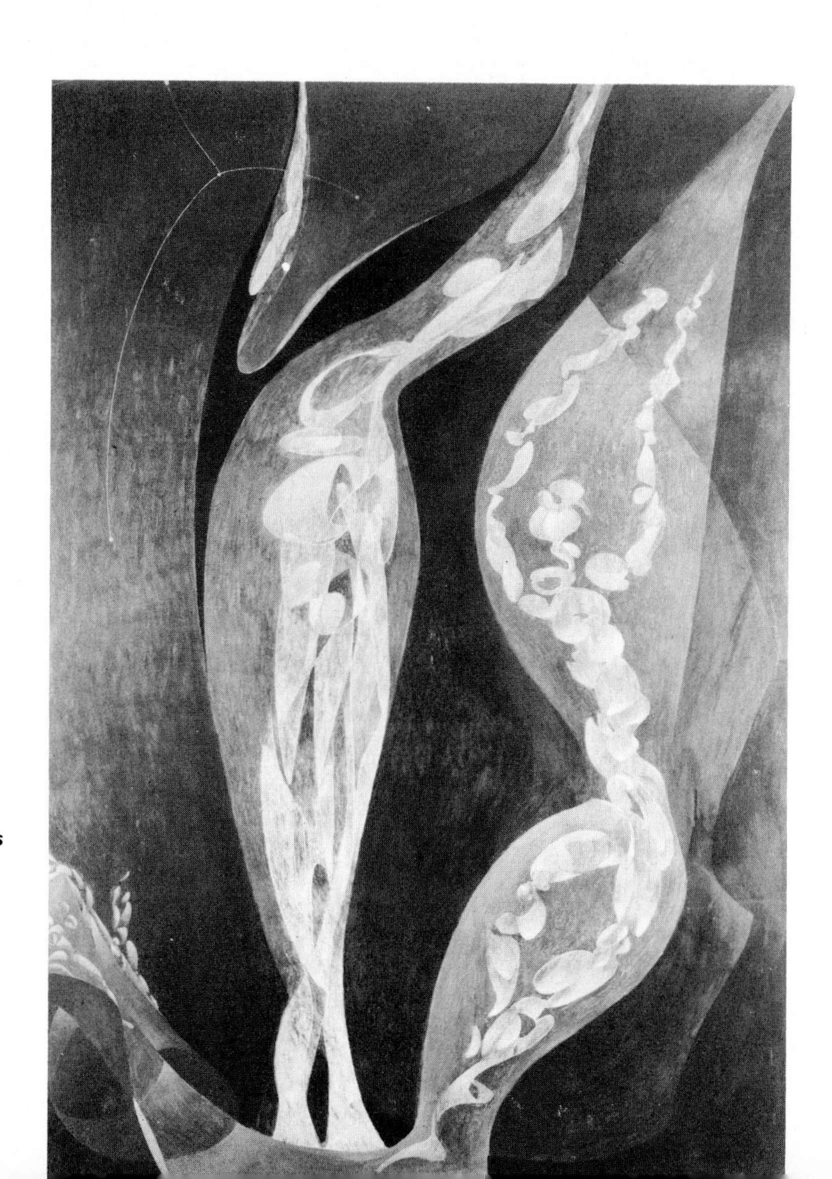

MAX ERNST *The Dancers*

BORIS MARGO *From a Cathedral*

PERMANENT OPINIONS

YESTERDAY AND TODAY

We are indebted to The Woodstock Artists Association for the following "Four Categories of Greatness" paraphrased from the book, *Principles of Chinese Painting.*

Paraphrased categories:

No. 1 The competent or clever artist. He works on the lowest level (!) of creation, possess skill and knows the rules of style. He can render "outward formal likeness" but his highest goal is only that of pleasing formal beauty.

No. 2 The cultivated painter. He is characterized by taste, can imbue technique with expressive power. He is called the *chi'i* (unusual) painter because "the things he makes are strange, queer and have neither reason nor resemblance." In other words, he has "brush, not thought."

No. 3 The divine or wonderful painter. He is the scholar-artist who begins to have "understanding of all things" and aims for artistic truth. For him the "inspiration of heaven is very high" and "the thoughts harmonize with the spirit."

No. 4 The supreme artist defies definition. "He grasps the self-existent, which cannot be imitated" and his work is marked by the absolute "wedding of spirit and matter." He is the genius and his is the freedom of effortless creation.

Eric Newton, in the Journal of Aesthetics and Art Criticism, compares the strata of form in the painters' work to layers of an onion. "They form a progression on the level of the skin, the artist is an observer; on the next level, that of the outer layer, he is a commentator; on the second layer he is an interpreter; on the third a visionary, and finally, when he reaches the core, a creator."

"A man having this ability to make beauty, which endures months of study and which does not decrease as you learn it more intimately, is what we call a great artist."

EZRA POUND

IN BOOK ON GAUDIA-BRZESKA

"We shall not be fully in control of our civilization, or able to express the qualities of life, until it is possible to reduce the tempo or accelerate it in response, not to the machine's requirements for production, but to man's requirements for a full and harmonious life." LEWIS MUMFORD

"The correct evaluation of the new is the prime test of the critic's merit." SAINTE-BEUVE

". . . there are few pleasures in art greater than the secure sense that one can recognize beauty when one comes upon it." AARON COPLAND

"Nature has seen fit that there shall be planted in every living creature an innate urge towards the larger life of the race."

JOSEPHINE A. JACKSON, M.D.

HELEN M. SALISBURY

"Criticism that is hostile or negative, even when it is good and well-founded, is seldom of any use to the artist himself as long as it remains impersonal." CHARLES MORGAN

"The critic is not to be regarded as a burden or a competitor to the artist but as an adjunct, someone by the artist's side, in a very real sense cooperating with the artist for the benefit of the community of which both artist and critic are a part." HAROLD CLURMAN

"I have neglected nothing." NICOLAS POUSSIN

"That is a fair working definition of magic, I think – something wonderful, incredible, the technique of which is hidden. The universe holds such magic. And poets, musicians, and artists whose techniques elude us, but whose work charms and thrills us, know something of its working." JENNETTE LEE
This Magic Body

"I offer some critical resolutions for the New Year. First, to speak favorably of whatever promising new work I am able to review within the limits of a monthly column. Second, not to speak unfavorably of what I do not like unless the artist already has an established reputation. Third, not to hesitate to attack an inflated reputation. Fourth to balance the claims of past and present. Fifth, to write for informed consumers, not producers, of art – on the theory that criticism has little reason to expect to influence an artist – who if he is any good, knows what he is about – and much reason to hope to develop a sympathetic audience for quality in art, wherever it may appear." S. LANE FAISON, JR.

"Our species is the only creative species, and it has only one creative instrument, the individual mind and spirit of a man. Nothing was ever created by two men. There are no good collaborations, whether in music, in art, in poetry, in mathematics, in philosophy. Once the miracle of creation has taken place, the group can build and extend it, but the group never invents anything. The preciousness lies in the lonely mind of a man." A writer's Credo
JOHN STEINBECK IN *East of Eden*

"Thinking is more interesting than knowing, but not so interesting as looking." GOETHE

"The only competition worthy of a wise man is with himself." ALLSTON

"We think, however, of cultural facts as they affect the lives of persons rather than as the deposit of greatness. For us, it is useful to admit the possibility that a second-rate art object may be either the cause or the effect of a first-rate experience, This is a hard doctrine for esthetes, but educators cannot escape it."
LYMAN BRYSON
The Drive Towards Reason.

"Art, unless quickened from above and from within, has in it nothing beyond itself which is visible beauty." JOHN BROWN

"To understand an artist's work it is necessary to follow him as far as possible into his home."
C. A. SAINT-BEUVE

"Each artist writes his own autobiography."
HAVELOCK ELLIS

"Art is made of knowledge, and the world of art is a system of knowledge as valuable to man – indeed more valuable – than the world of philosophy or the world of science."
HERBERT READ
Art and Society

RUTH ARMER *Abstraction No. 270*

ERLE LORAN *Under Sea*

EVERETT SPRUCE ***Precipice***

MAX WEBBER *Dauntless Bird*

MITCHELL JAMIESON

Maelstrom

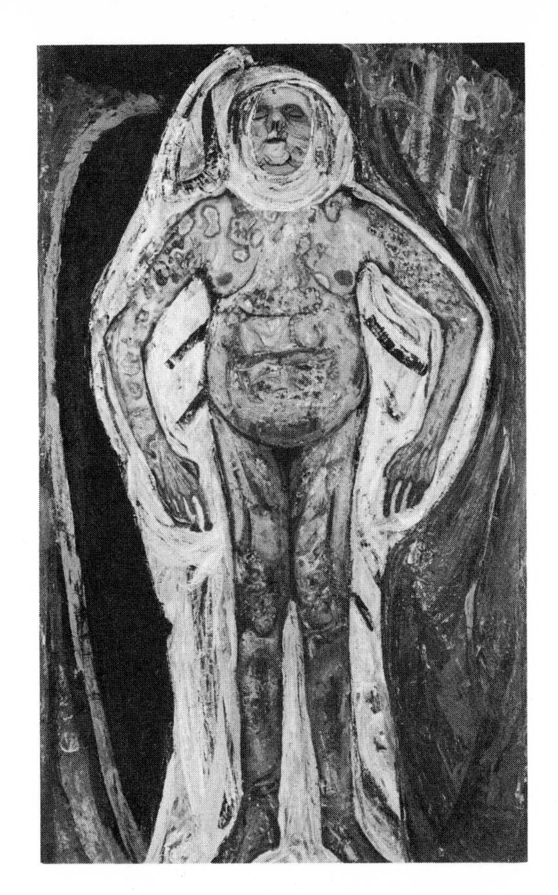

HYMAN BLOOM *Corpse of Elderly Female*

My work has continually been based upon a clue seen in nature from which the subject of a picture may be projected. Nature, with its profound order, is an inexhaustible source of supply. Its many facets lend themselves freely to all who would help themselves for their particular needs. CHARLES SHEELER

EDWARD MILLMAN *Invasion*

ROBERT MOTHERWELL *Wall Painting III*

Communication with painting is possible when the spectator shows an active and creative point of view, and he is not prejudiced or expecting to see objects in the picture representing natural forms. Often people ask what is modern painting and what does it mean? A well known painter once was asked if he could explain his paintings in words. He said if he would be able to do that and give a correct explanation, he would quit painting. Pictures are to be seen and felt, not to be explained. They speak for themselves.

JEAN XCERON

JIMMY ERNST *Personal Appearance*

I regret to add that I have no special credo to submit other than my passionate love of painting.

VACLAV VYTACIL

NILES SPENCER *In Fairmount*

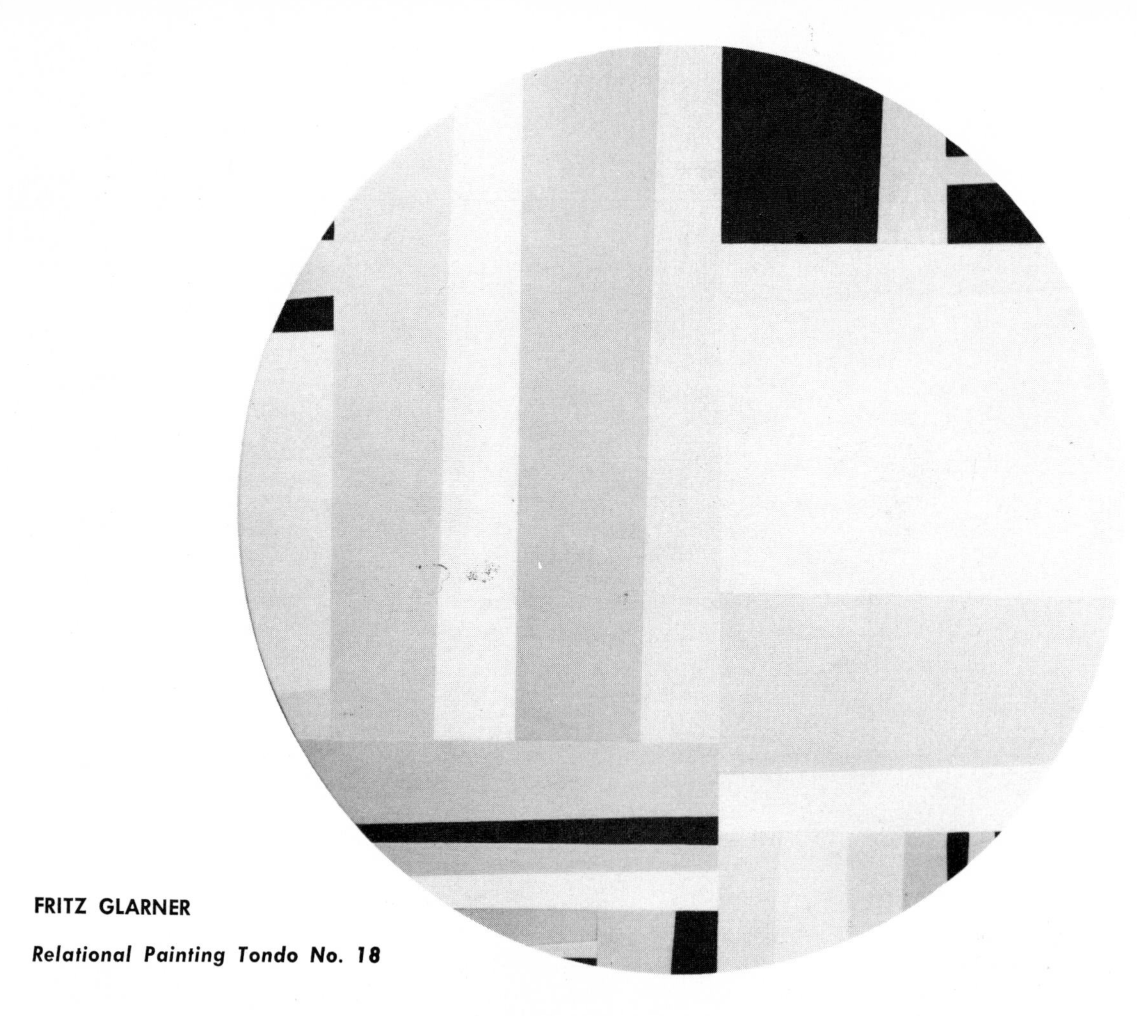

FRITZ GLARNER

Relational Painting Tondo No. 18

 JOHN BEAUCHAMP *Painting*

EDWARD HOPPER ***Rooms by the Sea***

JEAN XCERON ***Painting 341***

It can perhaps be assumed that no artist before Mondrian has ever set every portion of his canvas so harmoniously at rest. GEORGE L. K. MORRIS

YNEZ JOHNSTON *Black Palace with Red Courtyard*

GEORGIA O'KEEFFE *Early Spring Tree*

WILLIAM CONGDON ***Venice No. 1***

Painting is subject to human and not scientific laws, and art is not a great highway leading to utopias of style but rather documents of the most human need to contact other human beings in a way that is unique to art.

FRITZ BULTMAN

To lose oneself in the subject until it communicates to our subconscious an image specific enough to paint itself, so that when the painting is finished we, as many others, discover and marvel at its life. It is what the subject has done to us, the love, the image that it has created in us that we paint.

WILLIAM CONGDON

RICHARD HAINES *Night of Return*

ELWOOD GRAHAM *Spanish Lace*

There are idea painters and there are those who think or feel in paint . . . what intrigues and engages me is to captivate the sensual within a pointed aesthetic . . . two contrary elements, one to excite and the other to cool. The duality releases the need for thinking and feeling. PAUL BURLIN

ALFRED RUSSELL *Painting No. 24*

KENNETH CALLAHAN

Shadows on the Rock

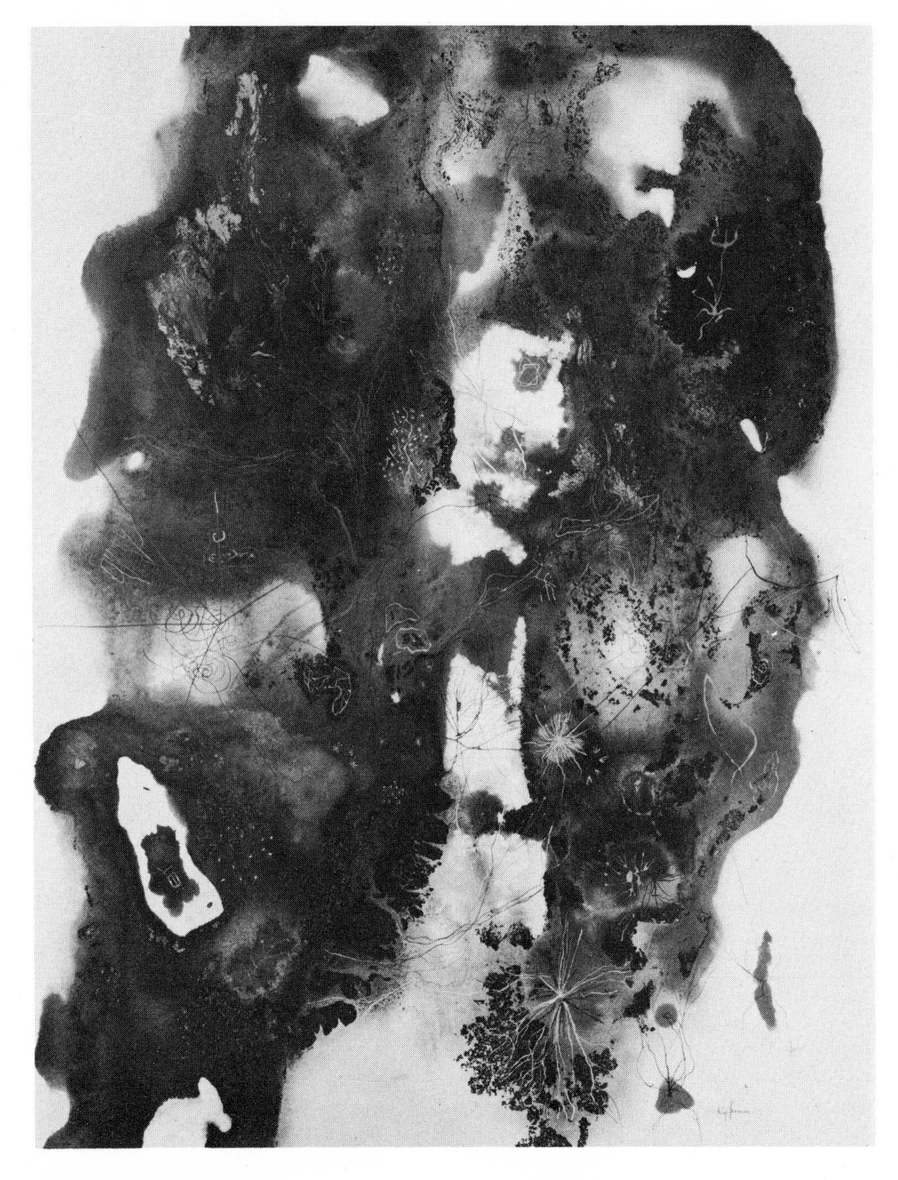

LAWRENCE KUPFERMAN ***Walden Pond***

A realm where the gestation and birth of plastic ideas are beyond the boundry of verbalization and are realized only through the articulation of pure painting.

ATTELIO SALEMME

BRADLEY WALKER TOMLIN *No. 3*

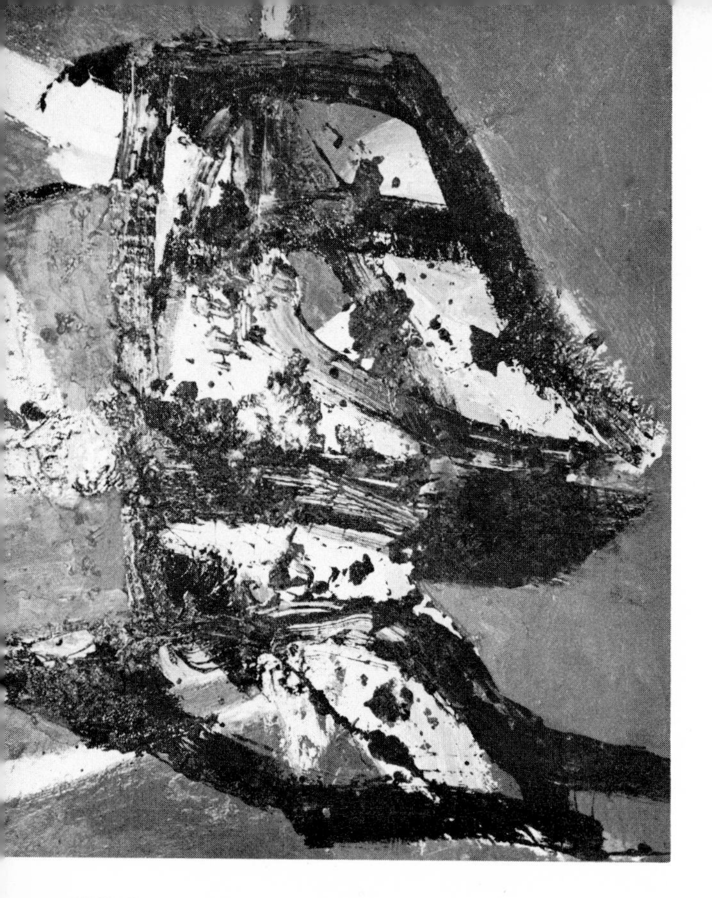

What is constant in art is the artist's description of himself and his environment. All that changes comes under the idea of form. It represents what one grasps of the new and hurls it into the past. Significant form is what lies outside the periphery of the known. An imaginative act is that which is capable of extending the periphery of the known till it includes the intuitively felt object that lies outside it. JACK TWORKOV

GEORGE McNEIL ***Painting***

SEYMOUR FOGEL ***Icarian Flight***

The landscape "Within Autumn" was compiled from various notes I made during October in New Hampshire. I hesitated to paint this as Autumn as it is so intensely colorful it seems uncontrollable and like most sunsets, it is better left to nature than man's translation.

FRANK D. DUNCAN

FELIX RUVOLD *Transcendental*

Painting to me is a means of realization — an awareness of things, not as a mirror to nature but as an articulation of man's intellectual-emotional response to life. To seize an experience, and involve it with feeling and form to such an intensity that it becomes a new experience, this is the joy of painting for me. RICHARD HAINES

KURT SELIGMANN *Effervescence No. 3*

AD REINHARDT ***No. 2***

I believe that abstract art stands eminently ahead of all other art today. Perhaps this is mainly due to the fact that the public in general takes comparatively little interest in it and consequently does not influence it. I have almost invariably found that those who object most to abstract art do so for wholly non-aesthetic reasons.

CHARLES G. SHAW

MILTON AVERY *Poetry after Breakfast*

BALCOMB GREENE *Nude in Yellow Ochre*

MICHAEL FRARY ***Apartment House***

My aim in painting has always been the most exact transcription of my most intimate impressions of nature. If this end is unattainable, so, it can be said, is perfection in any other ideal of painting, or in any other of man's activities.

EDWARD HOPPER

I believe in the dignity of honest work, and study to show myself approved unto God . . . a workman that need not be ashamed.

GEORGE BEATTIE, JR.

GREGORIO PRESTOPINO *Roots*

ATTILLIO SALEMME *The Sacrifice*

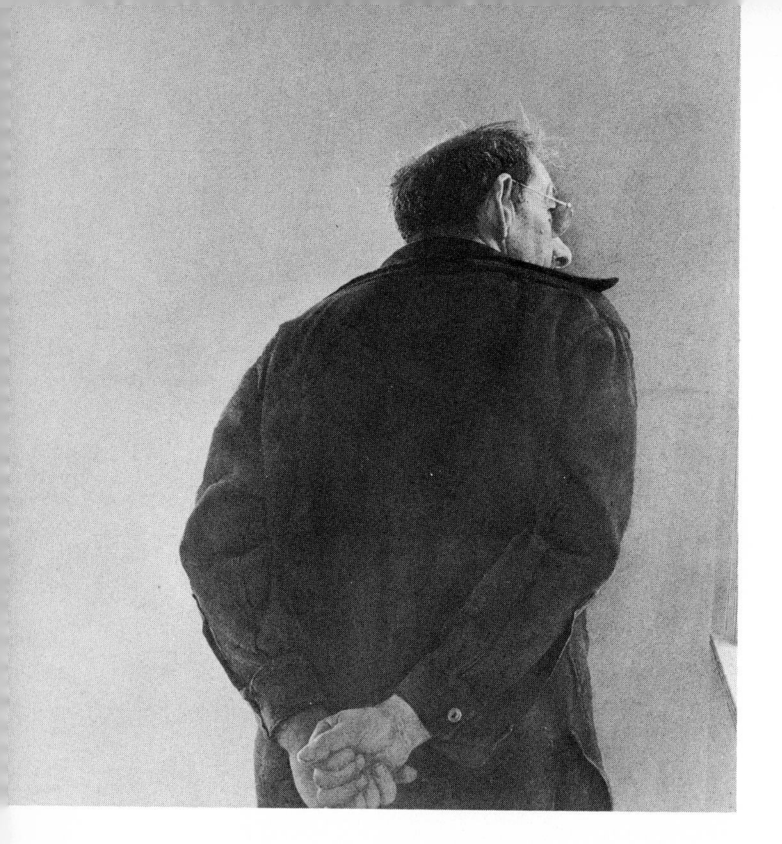

ANDREW WYETH *Man from Maine*

Painting is an independent plastic language. I try to express my feelings about the world in which I live — using control in a personal free way. The painting is the only thing that can "speak" for itself. GEORGE PICKEN

GEORGE GROSZ *A Dallas Night*

WILLIAM DODD *Monhegan Theme*

The good picture –
No one wonders at more than the one who created it.
Made . . . with an inborn instinct . . . in which time begets an awareness . . . and these periods of awareness are . . . The . . . red letter . . . days in the Creator's life. JOHN MARIN

BERNARD PERLIN *The Jacket*

BEN SHAHN ***Composition with 5 Clarinets and Tin Horn***

Painting is for me a problem of simultaneous understanding and explaining. I try to approach my subject uncluttered by aesthetic prejudices. I put it on canvas in order to explain it to myself, yet the result should reveal something plus.

HEDDA STERNE

LYONEL FEININGER *Lunar Web*

FRANKLIN C. WATKINS *Beloved Dead*

GEORGE L. K. MORRIS *Industrial Landscape*

ROBERT GWATHMEY *Winter's Playground*

Art is not just a language. It is more a process of osmosis of the tangible inner feelings of the artist to the inner feelings of the observer. It is the most direct means of communication of the hopes, ideals and dignity of mankind. Giotto, Piero della Francesca, Uccello, Breughel, Cezanne, Seurat and others are reassuring lights in the darkness of the wilderness.

MICHAEL FRARY

YVES TANQUY *Suites Illimitées*

DONG KINGMAN *Moon and Locomotive*

FRITZ BULTMAN *Sleeper*

PAUL BURLIN

The Magnificence

PHILIP EVERGOOD ***The Hunters***

I still believe the proper study of mankind is man, no matter how fascinating other excursions in art and science may be. I would like to see behind the surface of the canvas and see the man himself, his relationship to other men, to nature, to God. MITCHELL JAMIESON

The conflict between spontaneous and deliberate behavior, a great dualism of modern times, is felt keenly by the artist. It is also resolved most successfully by him because he deals with the actual form of the process of development, in which the static concepts of subject and object, spirit and matter, freedom and necessity, the immediate and tradition, have become harmless paradox.

JAMES BROOKS

FRANZ KLINE ***The Chief***

SYD SOLOMON ***Boca***

ART REFERENCE BRIEFS

NATIONAL ARTISTS ORGANIZATIONS

The following listing of artists and art organizations is presented not only for convenient reference, but as an indication of the wide scope of current professional activities in the field of art. Every effort has been made to insure accuracy, but the continual changes in personnel have made this very difficult. For this reason, the names of all officers except the secretary or executive director have been omitted.

ALLIED ARTISTS OF AMERICA

Address: 450 E. 63 St., New York, N. Y.
Corresponding secretary: David Humphreys
Organized 1914, incorporated 1922
Objective: The advancement of American art without antagonism to any existing institution.
Membership: About 300; only artists whose work has been accepted by the membership.
Activities: Annual exhibition.

AMERICAN ABSTRACT ARTISTS

Address: 30 Jones St., New York, N. Y.
Secretary: Ida Fischer
Established 1936
Objective: To unite American abstract artists; to bring their work to public attention; to foster appreciation of this direction in art.
Membership: Limited to 50; applicants submit examples of their work; dues $4.
Activities: Exhibitions, annual, several semi-annual; traveling shows throughout the U.S., in Europe and Japan; joint exhibitions invited with foreign groups; two books published.

AMERICAN ARTISTS PROFESSIONAL LEAGUE

National Arts Club Building, 15 Gramercy Park, New York, N. Y.
Executive Director: Gustave J. Noback
Established 1928; Slogan, "For American Art."
Membership: 1200; dues $6.50; self-governing chapters in states.
Activities: Conducts national exhibition; co-operates with national, state and local art and patriotic organizations; works for fair jury system, just copyright legislation, closing of fake galleries, permanent and guaranteed colors.

AMERICAN WATERCOLOR SOCIETY

Business office: 175 Fifth Ave., New York, N. Y.
Corresponding secretary: Cyril A. Lewis; executive secretary: Mary Colonna
Established 1866, incorporated 1903; New York Watercolor Club amalgamated with Society 1941.
Membership: 483; dues $5; nomination by Board of Control, based on excellence of work.
Activities: Annual exhibition, annual meeting.

ARTISTS EQUITY ASSOCIATION

13 East 67 St., New York, N. Y.
Executive director: Lincoln Rothschild
Established 1947
Objective: To promote and protect the economic interest of professional artists.
Membership: 2000; dues $12.
Activities: Publishes *Annual Directory of Open Exhibitions; Standard Artist-Dealer Form of Contract; Artistic Copyright* by Joshua B. Cahn; *Membership Newsletter.* Negotiates on behalf of profession as a whole with museums and dealers; commercial and institutional sponsors of art exhibitions and competitions. Promotes new opportunities for exhibitions of fine arts; government sponsorship of art on federal, state and municipal levels; education of public interest in American art; artists' personal welfare; international cultural relations; annual fund-raising ball.

ASSOCIATION OF ART MUSEUM DIRECTORS

Secretary-treasurer: Adelyn D. Breeskin, Baltimore Museum of Art, Baltimore, Md.
Established 1916
Membership: 68 active, 7 associate, 5 honorary.
Activities: Annual meeting for round table discussion of work of art museum executives.

AUDUBON ARTISTS

1083 Fifth Ave., New York, N. Y.
Established 1940 near site of Audubon homestead in New York.
Objective (from constitution): The advancement of art through exhibitions of work and by any other means that may seem desirable and proper.
Membership: 360.
Activities: Annual exhibition.

FEDERATION OF MODERN PAINTERS AND SCULPTORS

340 W. 72nd St., New York, N. Y.
Corresponding secretary: Elisabeth Model
Established 1940 to bring together outstanding painters and sculptors working in contem-

porary idioms for their common good.
Objectives: To present to the public authoritative works of modern art in its various aspects and forms.
Membership: Limited to about 100; dues $5.
Activities: Exhibitions, traveling exhibitions; forums; museum gift plan, endorsed museums throughout the United States, 16 gifts accepted in first year of plan.

NATIONAL ASSOCIATION OF WOMEN ARTISTS
67 East 59 St., New York, N. Y.
Executive Secretary: Mary K. Manning
Established 1889 as Women's Art Club of New York; known as National Association of Women Painters and Sculptors 1914-1941.
Membership: About 800 exhibitors in 44 states; dues, exhibitors $10 and $12, associates $10 and higher.
Activities: Annual exhibition in spring, awards, juries; operate Argent Galleries at above address; circulate shows, national and international.

NATIONAL SCULPTURE SOCIETY
1083 Fifth Ave., New York, N. Y.
Secretary: Frank Eliscu
Established 1893, incorporated 1896
Objective: "To foster the development and appreciation of sculpture in this country; and it is always ready to support any movement that furthers this cause."
Membership: Approximately 350; dues, fellows $15, members $10.
Activities: Exhibitions and competitions; administers trust fund; provides loans; publishes *National Sculpture Review.*

NATIONAL SERIGRAPH SOCIETY
38 West 57 St., New York, N. Y.
Director: Doris Meltzer
Established 1940, chartered by New York State Board of Regents and incorporated as an educational corporation 1945; federal tax free ruling 1948.
Membership: 75 artists; dues $25, foreign $35; associate membership open to public, dues $15; honorary associate membership $1000 or more annually.
Activities: Annual spring international exhibition of serigraphs, open to all artists; awards; permanent collection; circulates graphic exhibitions, classes; information center.

NATIONAL SOCIETY OF MURAL PAINTERS
1083 Fifth Ave., New York, N. Y.
Secretary: Cliff Young
Established and incorporated 1895
Objectives: To encourage and advance standards of mural painting in America; to formulate a code for decorative painting competitions in America and regulate professional practices.
Membership: 87; dues $10, non-resident $5.
Activities: Exhibitions from time to time with decorative and related arts; constituent member, Architectural League, Fine Arts Federation, Committee on Government and Art.

NATIONAL SOCIETY OF PAINTERS IN CASEIN
128 East 16 St., New York, N. Y.
Corresponding secretary: Ted Davis
Incorporated in New York in 1952
Purpose and scope: In most exhibitions casein is hung with watercolors or rejected because it is neither watercolor nor oil. The society wishes to give artists an opportunity to exhibit in casein no matter what the technique, style and general appearance may be.
Membership: Artists elected by membership committee; 60 members; dues $5, non-members entry fee $3.
Activities: Exhibitions, several at first for members only; first national exhibition 1955. Members jury-exempt; separate jury of awards.

SCULPTORS GUILD
96 Fifth Ave., New York, N. Y.
Executive Secretary: Cleo Hartwig
Established and incorporated 1937
Objective: To unite sculptors of progressive tendencies.
Membership: 88 professional sculptors in the United States; dues $12.
Activities: Annual exhibitions, outdoors if feasible.

SOCIETY OF AMERICAN GRAPHIC ARTISTS
1083 Fifth Ave., New York, N. Y.
Corresponding secretary: Sybilla Mittel Weber
Established 1915 as the Brooklyn Society of Etchers; incorporated 1931 as the Society of American Etchers, Inc.; scope broadened in 1947, and organization renamed Society of American Graphic Artists, Inc. in 1951.
Objectives: To promote the association of individuals interested especially in graphic arts and to advance interest in graphic arts.

Membership: About 220, associates 250; dues, artists $5, associates $10 (with print).
Activities: Meetings, spring and fall; annual exhibitions; permanent collection, other collections.

SOCIETY OF INDEPENDENT ARTISTS
215 West 57 St., New York, N. Y.
President: Stewart Klonis
Established 1917
Objective: To hold exhibitions without juries or prizes.
Membership: About 500 exhibitors and 100 associates.
Activities: Exhibitions open to all artists who pay entrance fee.

UNITED STATES COMMITTEE OF THE INTERNATIONAL ASSOCIATION OF PLASTIC ARTS
Studio 37, 58 West 57 St., New York, N. Y.
Secretary: Ruth Yates
Established 1955 to improve the economic and professional welfare of the artist, to develop public appreciation of contemporary art, and to speak for American artists at international congresses.
Membership: 13 leading national art societies charter members, open to established art societies, local and regional.
Activities: To establish clearing house information, conduct educational programs to interest artists and the public.

NATIONAL ART ORGANIZATIONS

AMERICAN ACADEMY OF ARTS AND LETTERS
633 West 155 St., New York, N. Y.
Secretary: Douglas Moore
Established 1904 by National Institute of Arts and Letters.
Membership: Limited to 50, chosen from Institute membership.
Activities: Public exhibitions, awards, public ceremonials.

AMERICAN FEDERATION OF ARTS
1083 Fifth Ave., New York, N. Y.
Director: Thomas M. Messer
Established 1909
Membership: Institutions, groups, individuals; open to anyone interested. Dues: Chapters $25; individuals $15.
Activities: Organizing and circulating domestic and foreign exhibitions of the fine arts and crafts. Publications sponsored: *Who's Who in American Art, American Art Directory, Art Newsletter* (monthly). Acts as clearing house for government and other agencies on art matters.

AMERICAN SOCIETY FOR AESTHETICS
Western Reserve University, Cleveland, Ohio
Secretary-treasurer: John F. White
Established 1942, affiliated with American Council of Learned Societies and International Federation of Philosophical Societies.
Objective: Advancement of philosophic and scientific studies of the arts and related fields.
Membership: 600; open to all interested; dues $6.
Activities: Holds annual national meeting; six regional divisions bring members together for seminars and informal discussions. Publishes quarterly *Journal of Aesthetics and Art Criticism* cooperatively with Cleveland Musum of Art and Western Reserve University.

COLLEGE ART ASSOCIATION OF AMERICA
432 Fourth Ave., New York, N. Y.
Business Manager: Peter Magill
Established 1912 by a group of professors.
Objectives: To raise standards of teaching and scholarship in the field of art; to promote study of art.
Membership: About 2600; classified; dues $12 up.
Activities: Annual meeting; book service; placement bureau; publishes *Art Bulletin* and *College Art Journal.*

LITURGICAL ARTS SOCIETY
7 East 42 St., New York, N. Y.
Secretary: Maurice Lavanoux
Founded by laymen, incorporated 1928. Nonprofit national organization under the patronage of His Eminence, Francis Cardinal Spellman.
Membership: Includes members of the American hierarchy, foreign prelates, members of the clergy and laity. Corporate membership dues $15, sustaining $10.
Activities: Society acts as center of information for promotion and spread of a proper concept of art as applied to Christian worship; publishes quarterly, *Liturgical Arts.*

NATIONAL ACADEMY OF DESIGN
1083 Fifth Ave., New York, N. Y.
Director: Vernon C. Porter
Established 1825, incorporated 1828
Membership: Painters (oil, watercolor); sculptors; graphic artists; architects.
Activities: Annual exhibitions, members and non-members; operates art school; administers two trust funds (Ranger for purchasing paintings, Abbey for commissions for murals).

NATIONAL ART EDUCATION ASSOCIATION
(A department of the NEA)
Address is that of the Secretary-treasurer: State Teachers College, Kutztown, Pennsylvania.
Secretary-treasurer: Horace F. Heilman
Established 1933; merging of four regional associations in the National Art Education Association, 1948.
Membership: 3909
Activities: Annual conference; publishes *Art Education.*

ART PERIODICALS

AMERICAN ARTIST. Monthly, illustrated. Ernest W. Watson, editor emeritus; Leighton Guptill, publisher; Norman Kent, editor; 24 West 40 st., New York, N. Y. Subscription $5 yearly, single copies $.60

AMERICAN ARTIST was founded in 1937 for the promotion of American art and artists. It serves the interest of both fine and commercial art and numbers among its readers painters, sculptors, printmakers, illustrators, advertising artists, art directors, teachers, students, craftsmen and writers.

Its policy is to reveal the artist's creative processes. Articles result chiefly from interviews, but some are written by artists. They take the reader behind the scenes, picturing steps in the projects, sometimes focusing on techniques, sometimes on creative aspects.

The "Taubes Page," a monthly discussion of the painter's craft, includes a question and answer column. The "Weathervane" surveys current trends. Otherwise the magazine does not attempt to cover news.

THE ART BULLETIN. Quarterly, illustrated. J. Carson Webster, editor-in-chief. Published by the College Art Association, 432 Fourth Ave., New York, N. Y. Included with membership in Association ($12) or subscription at same price to non-members. Single copies $3.

THE ART BULLETIN, now in its thirty-eighth volume, is devoted to scholarly articles and reviews on all periods of the history of art, or on the character and significance of individual work in its historical, cultural or formal aspects. Its editorial board is drawn from colleges and museums in America. Articles cover the art of any period, presenting the evidence available or new material, or clarifying or interpreting its development.

ART EDUCATION. Journal of the National Art Education Association, Eight issues yearly, illustrated. Dr. Jack Arends, editor, Teachers College, Columbia University, New York. Subscription to non-members $2

ART EDUCATION is the official organ of the National Art Education Association, a professional organization for all teachers and supervisors of art. It contains articles on philosophy and trends in art education by noted artists, educators, art supervisors and organization members, opinions being those of the writers and not necessarily of the Association.

The magazine has news of the four regional art education associations affiliated with the national; briefs on books and visual aids; information on happenings in art education.

ART IN AMERICA. Quarterly, illustrated, Jean Lipman, editor, Cannondale, Connecticut. Subscription $4, single copies $1. The new editorial board consists of top authorities in various fields of American art: Virgil Barker, John I. H. Baur, Louisa Dresser, Lloyd Goodrich, Talbot Hamlin, Bartlett H. Hayes, Jr., H. R. Hitchcock, Edgar Kaufmann, Jr., Katharine Kuh, Nina Fletcher Little, Dorothy C. Miller, E. W. Newton, Duncan Phillips, E. P. Richardson, James T. Soby, Gordon Washburn, Alice Winchester, Carl Zigrosser.

Founded in 1913, *ART IN AMERICA* is devoted to publication of scholarly articles in the field of American art, early and contemporary—painting, sculpture, architecture, graphic arts, decorative arts, American restorations, collecting American art. Articles present trends in contemporary art, collecting, museum policies, art criticism. There are features on American artists of all periods. Book-length monographs of this sort have been published on lesser-known and heretofore unpublished early American painters such as Winthrop Chandler, Duncanson, Gullagher, Hathaway, Savage and Ellsworth; and on contemporary painters such as Charles Sheeler. Book reviews, some illustrated, cover publications on early and contemporary American art. Outstanding authorities – critics, collectors, dealers, museum directors, research specialists – even best selling authors such as Kenneth Roberts – write for the magazine.

ART NEWS. Monthly, September to May; quarterly June, July, August. Alfred Frankfurter, editor; Thomas B. Hess, executive editor; Betty Chamberlain, managing editor. Published by The Art Foundation Press, Inc., 32 East 57th St., New York, N. Y. Subscription $9 without *ART NEWS ANNUAL,* a Christmas supplement; $11.75 with *ANNUAL;* single copies $1. Founded in 1902, *ART NEWS* is America's oldest art magazine. With circulation over the 40,000 mark it serves a national and international audience with factual coverage of events in the art field as well as with articles by scholars and artists on all phases of ancient and modern art. *ART NEWS* began as a weekly broadside to guide "art editors and collectors concerning artists, art exhibitions and sales of art objects." The monthly now runs to 72 pages and over. *ART NEWS ANNUAL,* which regularly contains more than 40 colorplates, is distributed through regular hard-cover book channels (by Simon & Schuster). In June 1953 the *ART NEWS* absorbed the circulation of the *MAGAZINE OF ART.*

The magazine has a three-fold purpose: 1) reviewing exhibitions, sales, museum acquisitions, art events; 2) major articles by widely known critics, scholars, historians and artists, and features such as the "Paints a Picture" series; 3) editorials (usually by the editor) on a wide range of topics. Although *ART NEWS* champions no particular school of contemporary art, it gives full and sympathetic coverage to the *avant-garde.*

THE ART QUARTERLY. Illustrated. W. R. Valentiner and E. P. Richardson, editors. Published by the Detroit Institute of Arts. Subscription $5 yearly, single copies $1.25.

THE ART QUARTERLY is the leading magazine in the scholarship of art published in America, and the only one written for collectors and connoisseurs as well as historians. It appeared first in 1938, consists of 90-100 pages with thirty or more sharply detailed half-tone illustrations. In the field of ancient and modern art it publishes articles from the American viewpoint of art history, connoisseurship and development of ideas. Contributors are chiefly American but include English, French, Italian and Austrian scholars, and museum personnel. There are short notes on individual works of art, a review of acquisitions by American museums, a section devoted to the publication of drawings, and reviews of books on art.

ARTS. Incorporating *ART DIGEST.* Published semi-monthly October through May, monthly June through September, by The Art Digest, Inc., 116 E. 59 St., New York, N. Y. Jonathan Marshall, editor. Subscription $5, single copies $.50 Founded in 1926 by Peyton Boswell, *ARTS* takes the professional art world as its province. These features appear regularly in *ARTS:* Great Masters Section – from Michelangelo to Matisse. Intimate Profiles of Today's Outstanding Artists. Up-to-the-Minute News and Reviews of the Art World. Useful Art Techniques – new materials – where to show. Exclusive Tours through Museums and Private Collections. Also – unusual discoveries – special articles – auction news – book reviews – a complete calendar of events.

COLLEGE ART JOURNAL. Quarterly. Henry R. Hope, editor-in-chief. Published by the College Art Association, 432 Fourth Ave., New York, N. Y. Subscription $2, single copies $.50. The only quarterly dealing primarily with the problems of teaching art, the *COLLEGE ART JOURNAL* is now in its fifteenth volume. It contains short articles on fundamental questions in education, and is a forum for open discussion, news and summaries of activities of art departments, museums and the interests of the Association. Readers, over 2500 members of the College Art Association, in universities, colleges and art schools.

JOURNAL OF AESTHETICS AND ART CRITICISM. Quarterly. Thomas Munro, editor. Published by the American Society for Aesthetics. Address of editor, Cleveland Museum of Art, Cleveland, Ohio. Subscription $6 yearly, single copies $2.

THE JOURNAL OF AESTHETICS AND ART CRITICISM is the only periodical in

English devoted to theoretical discussion of the arts and related modes of experience. It presents scholarly discussions of all the arts, of aesthetics, of art education, and of the philosophy, psychology and sociology of art. It reaches members of the American Society for Aesthetics, individual subscribers, and libraries in the United States and thirty-nine foreign countries. The Journal offers an opportunity to exchange ideas with persons of similar interests and to combine findings. It acts as liaison between the Society and foreign societies. Its office is an international center for correspondence and discussion among scholars interested in theoretical studies of the arts. Many articles by foreign scholars are published. Articles by its American authors have been translated into foreign languages.

Seventeen institutions, besides the Cleveland Museum of Art and Western Reserve University, sponsor the Journal each year. Book reviews, a current bibliography, news notes and international correspondence are features.

LITURGICAL ARTS, A Quarterly Devoted to the Arts of the Catholic Church. Illustrated. Maurice Lavanoux, managaging editor. Published by the Liturgical Arts Society, Inc. Editorial offices, 7 East 42 St., New York, N. Y. Subscription $5, single copies $1.25. Quarterly sent to all members.

LITURGICAL ARTS, now in its twenty-fourth volume, contains articles and illustrations dealing with the planning, building and decoration of churches and all ancillary structures; the renovation and remodeling of existing buildings; the design and execution of sacred vessels, vestments, sculpture, and painting; also articles on music and other matters subject to liturgical usage. Books relating to these subjects are reviewed and appraised; significant events and tendencies are discussed.

PICTURES ON EXHIBIT. Monthly (10 issues). Illustrated. Charles Z. Offin, editor-in-chief. Pictures Publishing Co., 30 East 60 St., New York, N. Y. Subscription $3, single copies $.35.

PICTURES ON EXHIBIT was established in 1937 to meet the interests and needs of the rapidly growing segment of the public that was attending, in increasingly large numbers, the art exhibits held throughout the country. Designed in a handy, compact format, pocket-size, emphasizing conciseness and clarity of language and illustrated with over thirty handsomely printed reproductions, its editorial formula has proved to be as useful to the busy art museum official as to the layman who wants to know what is going on in the art world.

In addition to its critical previews of art shows in New York and other cities, the magazine maintains regular sections devoted to exhibits in Paris, London, Rome, Zurich, and Mexico City, in each of which cities it has an editor. This world-wide coverage was developed immediately after the close of World War II.

SCHOOL ARTS. Monthly, ten issues, illustrated. Kenneth Winebrenner, editor (address 400 Woodland Drive, Buffalo). Published at Printers Building, Worcester, Mass. Subscription $5, single copies $.75.

Now in its fifty-sixth year, *SCHOOL ARTS* is the pioneer art education magazine in America. It serves as a teaching aid for pre-school age to art school and college. Much material is appropriate for professionals and amateurs.

Leading artists and art educators contribute articles with emphasis on the practical approach, which introduces the reader to various materials and processes. Creative work is stressed. An effort is made to keep the articles well balanced between two-dimensional and three-dimensional art activities, with something of interest on different levels. Book reviews, general information and reports on activities of art organizations are included. Recent changes include an improved format with large bleed photographs. A new group of advisory editors has leading educators and teachers from the United States and Canada.

SUGGESTED READING

Compiled by Muriel Baldwin, formerly Chief, Art and Architecture Division, New York Public Library. This list of recent and standard books, selected for their range of information, may be useful as a guide to background reading in contemporary art.

Arnheim, Rudolf
Art and visual perception, a psychology of the creative age. Berkeley & Los Angeles. University of California Press. 1954. 408 p.

Barker, Virgil
American painting, history and interpretation. New York. Macmillan Co. 1950. 717 p.

Baur, John I. H.
Revolution and tradition in modern American art. Cambridge, Mass. Harvard University Pres. 1951. 170 p.

Bazin, Germain
History of modern painting; published under the supervision of Germain Bazin, translated from the French by Rosamund Frost. New York. Hyperion Press. 1951. 391 p.

Beigel, Hugo G.
Wake up to art. New York. Stephen Daye Press. 1950. 352 p.

Bell, David
The language of pictures. London, B. T. Batsford, Ltd. 1953. 162 p.

Berkman, Aaron
Art and space. New York. Social Sciences Publications. 1949. 175 p.

Bethers, Ray
How paintings happen, with diagrams by the author. New York. W. W. Norton & Co. 1951. 150 p.

Biederman, Charles
Letters on the new art and art as the evolution of visual knowledge. Red Wing, Minn. Charles Biederman, 1951. 91 p.

Blanshard, Frances Bradshaw
Retreat from likeness in the theory of painting. 2nd rev. & enl. ed. New York. Columbia University Pres. 1949. 178 p.

Boas, Franz
Primitive art. Irvington-on-Hudson, Capitol Publishing Co. 1951. 376 p.

Boas, George
Wingless Pegasus, a handbook for critics. Baltimore. John Hopkins Press. 1950. 244 p.

Flanagan, George A.
How to understand modern art. New York. The Studio Publications, Inc. in association with Thomas Y. Crowell Company. 1951. 334 p.

Goldscheider, Ludwig, ed.
Towards modern art or: King Solomon's picture book, art of the new age and art of former ages shown side by side. New York. Phaidon. 1952. 98 pls.

Gombrich, Ernest H.
The story of art. New York. Phaidon Publishers. 1950. 462 p.

Hess, Thomas B.
Abstract painting; background and American phase. New York. The Viking Press. 1951. 164 p.

Kuh, Katherine
Art has many faces. The nature of art presented visually. New York. Harper & Brothers. 1951. 185 p.

Larkin, Oliver W.
Art and life in America. New York. Rinehart. 1949. 547 p.

Lassaigne, Jacques
Painters of the twentieth century, cubism and fantastic art. Geneva and New York. Skira. 1952. (Skira color prints) 16 color plates with descriptive text.

Leenhardt, Maurice
Arts of the Oceanic peoples. London. Thames & Hudson. 1950. 124 p.

Leepa, Allen
The challenge of modern art, with a foreword by Herbert Read. New York. The Beechhurst Press. 1949. 256 p.

Lynes, Russell
The tastemakers. New York. Harper. 1954 362 p.

Malraux, André
The voices of silence. Translated by Stuart Gilbert. Garden City. Doubleday. 1953. 661 p.

Metropolitan Museum of Art, New York
American painting of today, a national competitive exhibition, 1950. New York. Metropolitan Museum of New York. 1950. Text and pls. (52)

Metropolitan Museum of Art, New York.
100 American painters of the 20th century, works selected from the collections of the

Metropolitan Museum of Art, with an introduction by Robert Beverly Hale. New York. Metropolitan Museum of Art. 1950. Text and 111 pls.

Modern artists in America: first series, 1949/50. Editorial Associates, Robert Motherwell, Ad Reinhart. New York. Wittenborn, Schultz, Inc. 1951. 388 p. (Documents of Modern Art.)

Motherwell, Robert, editor.
The Dada painters & poets: an anthology. New York. Wittenborn, Schultz Inc. 1951. 388 p. (Documents of Modern Art.)

Munsterberg, Hugo
Twentieth century painting. New York. Philosophical Library. 1951. 102 p.

Myers, Bernard S.
Modern art in the making. New York. McGraw-Hill Book Co. Inc. 1950. 457 p.

New York (City). Museum of Modern Art.
Abstract painting and sculpture in America. New York. Museum of Modern Art. 1951. 159 p.

New York (City). Museum of Modern Art.
Fantastic art, dada, surrealism, edited by Alfred H. Barr, Jr.; essays by George Hunet. New York. The Museum of Modern Art. Distributed by Simon and Schuster. 1947. 271 p.

New York (City). Museum of Modern Art.
Masters of modern art. Edited by Alfred H. Barr, Jr. New York. Distributed by Simon and Schuster. 1954. 239 p.

Ozenfant, Amédée
Foundations of modern art. Translated by John Rodker. Rev. ed. N. Y. Dover Publications 1952. 323 p.

Pearson, Ralph M.
Modern renaissance in American art; presenting the work and philosophy of 54 distinguished artists. New York. Harper. 1954. 300 p.

Pepper, Stephen Coburn
Principles of art appreciation. New York. Harcourt, Brace. 1949. 326 p.

Rathbun, Mary Chalmers
Layman's guide to modern art; painting for a scientific age [by] Mary Chalmers Rathbun [and] Bartlett H. Hayes, Jr. New York. Oxford University Press. 1949. unpaged.

Raynal, Maurice
History of modern painting. Tranlated by Gilbert Stuart. Geneva. Skira. 1949-1950. 3 vols.
Vol. I. From Baudelaire to Bonnard.
Vol. II. Matisse, Munch, Rouault, Fauvism, Expressionism.
Vol. III. From Picasso to Surrealism.

Read, Herbert Edward
Art now; an introduction to the theory of modern painting and sculpture. Rev. and enl. ed. London. Faber and Faber. 1948. 144 p.

Read, Herbert
The philosophy of modern art; collected essays London. Faber and Faber. 1952. 278 p.

Robb, David Metheny
The Harper history of painting, the Occidental tradition. New York. Harper & Bros. 1951. 1006 p.

Sachs, Paul J.
Modern prints and drawings; a guide to a better understanding of modern draughtsmanship; selected with an explanatory text by Paul J. Sachs. New York. Alfred A. Knopf. 1954. 261 p.

Soby, James Thrall
Contemporary painters. New York. Museum of Modern Art. 1948. 151 p.

Three lectures on modern art . . . By Katherine S. Dreier; . . . James Johnson Sweeney . . . Naum Gabo . . . New York. Philosophical Library. 1949. 91 p.

Upjohn, Everard Miller
History of the world art [by] Everard M. Upjohn, Paul S. Wingert [and] Jane Gaston Mahler. New York. Oxford University Press. 1949.

Venturi, Lionello
Impressionists and symbolists. Translated by Francis Steegmuller. New York. Scribner. 1950.

Whitney Museum of American Art, New York
Exhibition of contemporary American painting. New York. Whitney Museum of American Art. (Annual: title varies.)

Wight, Frederick S.
Milestones of American painting in our century. New York. Chanticleer Press. 1949.

Wilenski, Reginald Howard
Modern movement in art. London. Faber & Faber. 1945. 210 p.

Zaidenberg, Arthur, compiler
The art of the artist; theories and techniques of art by the artists themselves. New York. Crown Publishers. 1951. 176 p.

Zucker, Paul
Styles in painting, a comparative study. New York. Viking. 1950. 338 p.

REFERENCE INDEX AND CREDITS

Artists, Galleries, Museums and Collectors

We wish to express our genuine appreciation to everyone who has helped to make this book possible. Our gratitude is especially extended to all the artists, museum directors, gallery directors and individual collectors, who have enthusiastically participated.

PAGE	ARTIST
24 & JACKET	Adler, Samuel M: *Invocation,* (1952, oil, 30″ by 42″) Owned by Whitney Museum of American Art, Courtesy Grace Borgenicht Gallery.
42	Albers, Joseph: *Homage to the Square,* (1950, oil) Courtesy Sidney Janis Gallery.
44	Albright, Ivan: *The Wild Bunch,* (oil, 1950-1951) Courtesy The Museum of Modern Art.
48	Anderson, John: *Creation of Eve,* (oil) Courtesy Hacker Gallery.
86	Armer, Ruth: *Abstraction No. 270,* (oil, 1951, 24″ by 30″) Courtesy San Francisco Museum of Art.
72	Atherton, John: *Rocky Farmyard,* (water color, 1951, 16″ by 20″) Courtesy Associated American Artists.
103	Avery, Milton: *Poetry after Breakfast,* (oil, 40″ by 50″, 1951) Courtesy Grace Borgenicht Gallery.
82	Baziotes, William: *Jungle,* (oil, 50″ by 60″ 1951) Courtesy Samuel M. Kootz Gallery, Collection Mrs. Nelson A. Rockefeller.
26	Beattie, Jr. George: *Pisa* (gouache, 1952) Collection James H. Grady, Courtesy The Cleveland Museum of Art.
92	Beauchamp, John: *Painting* (lacquer on fabricated board, 29⅞″ by 40¼″, 1951) Courtesy Whitney Museum of American Art.
61	Benrimo, Tom: *Reflections* (oil, 24″ by 30″ 1951-52) Collection Mr. William Scott, Courtesy Fort Worth Art Center.
89	Bloom, Hyman: *Corpse of Elderly Female,* Collection Mr. Kirk Askew of Durlacher Bros.
67	Blume, Peter: *Crucifixion,* Courtesy Durlacher Bros.
75	Booth, Cameron: *Evening,* (oil, 25″ by 38″ 1947-50) Courtesy Bertha Shaefer Gallery.
78	Bouche, Louis: *High Street, Bus Barn,* (oil 20″ by 24″, 1952) Courtesy Kraushaar Gallery.
48	Brice, William: *Rose Sequence,* (oil, 93½″ by 27½″, 1952) Courtesy Downtown Gallery.
68	Brook, Alexander: *Remnants,* (oil) Collection Arizona State College, Courtesy Frank K. M. Rehn Gallery.
63	Brook, James: *No. 44,* (oil, 33½″ by 59″, 1951) Courtesy Grace Borgenicht Gallery.
22	Brown, Byron: *Azoic Fugue,* (oil, 24″ by 30″, 1952) Owned by Mr. and Mrs. J. F. Hood, Courtesy Grand Central Moderns.
61	Browne, Carlyle: *Table with Glasses and Roses* (oil, 36″ by 40″, 1951) Collection University of Illinois, Courtesy Catherine Viviano Gallery.
69	Buck, Lewis: *Iotrio* (oil, 18″ by 34″, 1951) Collection Linden Gallery of Contemporary Art, Courtesy Virginia Museum of Fine Art.
112	Bultman, Fritz: *Sleeper,* (oil, 30″ by 38″, 1952) Collection Whitney Museum of American Art, Courtesy Samuel M. Kootz Gallery.
41	Burchfield, Charles: *Sun and Rocks,* (watercolor) Courtesy Frank K. M. Rehn Gallery.
112	Burlin, Paul: *The Magnificence,* (oil, 50″ by 40″, 1952) Courtesy Downtown Gallery.
97	Callahan, Kenneth: *Shadows on Rock* (oil, 48″ by 36″, 1951-52) Courtesy Seattle Art Museum and Maynard Walker Gallery.
20	Cavallion, Giorgio: *Abstract No. 6,* (oil, 1952) Courtesy Egan Gallery.
95	Congdon, William: *Venice No. 1,* (oil, 48″ by 40″, 1951) Courtesy City Art Museum and Betty Parsons Gallery.
40	Cook, Howard: *Bridge No. 1,* (oil, 30″ by 48″, 1950) Collection Philadelphia Museum of Art, Courtesy Grand Central Moderns.
73	Connelly, Brian: *Attraction* (oil, 16″ by 20″, 1950) Collection the Art Institute of Chicago.
66	Davis, Stuart: *Tournos,* Collection Munson Williams Proctor Institute, Utica, N. Y.
50	de Kooning, William: *Excavation* (oil on canvas, 68⅛″ by 8′ 4½″)
63	Dehn, Adolf: *Haitian Heaven* (oil, 48″ by 30″, 1951) Collection Dr. and Mrs. Herman Schildkraut, Courtesy Associated American Artists.

PAGE ARTIST

18 Dickinson, Edwin: *Ruin at Daphne,* Courtesy The Metropolitan Museum of Art (60″ by 48″).

107 Dodd, William: *Monhegan Theme,* (oil, 24″ by 36″, 1950) Collection Metropolitan Museum of Art, Courtesy Grand Central Moderns.

23 Dozier, Otis: *Passage to the Sea* (oil, 24″ by 36″, 1952) Courtesy Fort Worth Art Center and Mortimer Levitt Gallery.

59 Duncan, Frank: *Within Autumn,* (oil, 26″ by 33″) Collection of Durlacher Bros.

47 Ellis, Dean: *Scrap,* (oil and wax, 1952) Collection Cleveland Museum of Art, Norman O. Stone and Ella A. Stone Memorial, Courtesy Grand Central Moderns.

91 Ernst, Jimmy: *Personal Appearance,* (oil, 35½″ by 47¾″, 1952) Courtesy Grace Borgenicht Gallery.

82 Ernst, Max: *The Dancers,* (oil, 1951) Courtesy Alexander Tolos Gallery.

113 Evergood, Philip: *The Hunters* (oil) Collection A.C.A. Gallery.

46 Farr, Charles, Griffen: *A Street in Knoxville,* (oil, 24″ by 30″) Courtesy San Francisco Museum of Art and Rotunda Gallery.

109 Feininger, Lyonel: *Lunar Web,* (oil, 21″ by 36″, 1951) Collection Mr. Milton Loewenthal, Courtesy Curt Valentine Gallery Inc.

79 Finch, Keith: *Locomotive,* (oil, 72″ by 48″, 1952) Courtesy Los Angeles County Museum and Landau Gallery.

104 Frary, Michael: *Apartment House,* (oil, 1952) Courtesy Dallas Museum of Fine Arts and Betty McLean Gallery.

60 Friebert, Joseph: *Synagogue,* (oil, 24″ by 48″, 1952) Courtesy The Art Institute of Chicago, Owned by Dr. and Mrs. A. Melamed.

100 Fogel, Seymour: *Icarian Flight,* (oil, 48″ by 72″) 1951-52, Courtesy Fort Worth Art Center and Betty McLean Gallery.

80 Gaertner, Carl: *Bend in Storm King,* (water color, 24″ by 40″, 1949-50, Died in 1952) Courtesy The Cleveland Museum of Art, Collection Adelle.

16 Gatch, Lee: *The Flame* 1950 Courtesy Newman Gallery.

64 Gibran, Kahlil: *The China Shop,* (oil on canvas, 36″ by 22″, 1948) Courtesy Institute of Contemporary Art and Margaret Brown Gallery.

92 Glarner, Fritz: *Relational Painting, Tondo No. 18* (oil on Masonite, 47½″ diam. 1950-51) Collection Dr. and Mrs. S. Lichterman, Courtesy Rose Fried Gallery.

25 Gonzales, Xavier: *Landscape,* (oil) Courtesy Grand Central Moderns.

FACING 32 Gorky, Arshile: *Betrothal II,* Collection of the Whitney Museum of American Art, New York.

PAGE ARTIST

65 Gottlieb, Adolph: *The Frozen Sounds,* (oil, 36″ by 48″, 1951) Courtesy Samuel M. Kootz Gallery.

96 Graham, Elwood: *Spanish Lace,* (oil, 1949) Gift of Mr. and Mrs. A. K. Salz to San Francisco Museum of Art, permanent collection.

103 Greene, Balcomb: *Nude in Yellow Ochre,* (oil, 36″ by 48″, 1951-52) Courtesy Bertha Schaefer Gallery.

106 Grosz, George: *A Dallas Night* (water color) Courtesy Associated American Artists.

17 Graves, Morris: *Preening Sparrows,* (oil, 52″ by 22″, 1952) Collins and Moffet Collection. Courtesy Seattle Art Museum and Willard Gallery.

110 Gwathmey, Robert: *Winter's Playground,* (oil, 25½″ by 36″) Courtesy A.C.A. Gallery.

96 Haines, Richard: *Night of Return,* (oil, 30″ by 40″) Courtesy Dalzell, Hatfield Galleries, in a private collection.

55 Hanson, Joseph M: *Composition,* (oil) Courtesy Passedoit Gallery.

60 Heliker, John: *Palazzo* (oil, 30″ by 24″, 1950) Collection of George S. Peer, Courtesy Kraushaar Galleries.

71 Halsey, William M.: *The Onlookers,* (oil, 20″ by 24″, 1951) Collection Mr. and Mrs. Joseph D. Read, Courtesy Bertha Schaefer Gallery.

93 Hopper, Edward: *Rooms by the Sea,* (oil, 48″ by 60″, 1951) Collection Mr. Fred Olsen, Courtesy Samuel M. Kootz Gallery.

65 Hofman, Hans: *Blue Enchantment,* (oil) Samuel M. Kootz Gallery.

88 Jamieson, Mitchell: *Maelstrom,* (encaustic, 30″ by 36″, 1951) Courtesy Seattle Art Museum and Maynard Walker Gallery.

94 Johnston, Ynez: *Black Palace with Red Courtyard* (casein, 25″ by 40″. 1952) Collection. Wadsworth Atheneum, Courtesy Paul Kantor Gallery.

FACING 50 Kantor, Morris: *The Summertime.* Courtesy Frank K. M. Rehn Gallery.

76 Karfoil, Bernard: *Repose,* (oil) Courtesy The Downtown Gallery, owned by this gallery.

70 Kienbusch, William: *Twin Pine* (casein, 26″ by 39″) Collection Whitney Museum of American Art, Courtesy Kraushaar Galleries.

64 Katzman Herbert: *Two Nudes Before Japanese Screen,* (oil on masonite) Courtesy Downtown Gallery.

111 Kingman, Dong: *Moon and Locomotive* (water color, 24″ by 30″) Collection Coca-Cola Bottling Co. Courtesy Midtown Galleries.

114 Kline, Franz: *The Chief,* (oil on canvas, 58⅜″ by 73½″, 1950) Collection Museum of Modern Art, gift of Mr. and Mrs. David Solinger.

PAGE ARTIST

70 Knaths, Karl: *Red Clock,* (oil, 40″ by 30″, 1952) Collection Joseph H. Hirshborn, Courtesy Paul Rosenberg and Co.

98 Kupferman, Lawrence: *Walden Pond,* Courtesy Mortimer Levitt Gallery.

95 Kuniyoshi, Yasuo: *Amazing Juggler,* (oil, 40″ by 65″, 1952) Collection of the Downtown Gallery.

37 Lebrun, Rico: *Rooster on the Arm of the Cross,* (oil, 35″ by 48″, 1952) Courtesy City Art Museum of St. Louis and Jacques Seligman and Co.

27 Leonid: *Provincetown,* (oil, 50″ by 32″, 1950) Owned by Durlacher Brothers.

77 Lester, William: *Old Fort Davies, Two Story,* (oil, 24″ by 30″, 1950) Courtesy Fort Worth Art Center and Passedoit Gallery.

59 Lewandouski, Edmund D.: *Gulf Coast Shipyard,* (oil, 26″ by 32″, 1951) Courtesy Virginia Museum and Downtown Gallery.

75 Levine, Jack: *Under the El,* (oil, 36″ by 58″, 1952) Colection Phillips Gallery, Courtesy Downtown Gallery.

86 Loran, Erle: *Under Sea,* (gouache, 15″ by 30″, 1952) Courtesy San Francisco Museum of Art and Catherine Viviano Gallery.

55 Lundeberg, Helen: *The Mirror,* (oil, 30″ by 36″, 1950) Courtesy Los Angeles County Museum.

4 MacIver, Loren: *Spatters and Leaves,* (oil on canvas, 25¾″ by 56″, 1950) Collection Mrs. G. MacCullock, Courtesy Pierre Matisse Gallery.

100 McNeil, George: *Painting,* (oil, 32″ by 40″, 1952) Courtesy Egan Gallery.

21 McFee, Henry: *Things on a Table,* (oil) Courtesy Frank K. M. Rehn, Collection Millard Sheets.

83 Margo, Boris: *From a Cathedral,* (oil, 26″ by 30″, 1950) Courtesy Betty Parsons Gallery.

FACING 16 Marin, John: *Sunset,* (watercolor, 17¼″ x 22¼″) Collection Mrs. Edith Gregor Halpert, Courtesy of The Downtown Gallery.

76 Mattson, Henry: *Headland,* (oil, 20″ by 28″, 1951) Courtesy Frank K. M. Rehn Galleries.

24 Menkes, Sigmund: *Boy Playing Harmonica,* (oil) Courtesy Museum of Modern Art.

89 Millman, Edward: *Invasion,* (oil 30″ by 60″, 1952) Collection Downtown Gallery.

52 Morgan, Maude: *Descension,* (oil, 27½″ by 42″, 1949-50) Courtesy Betty Parsons Gallery.

90 Motherwell, Robert: *Wall Painting III,* (oil, 48″ by 72″) Courtesy Kootz Gallery.

80 Morris, Carl: *Riders, No. 10,* (casein, 33″ by 27″, 1951) Courtesy Seattle Art Museum and Kraushaar Galleries.

PAGE ARTIST

110 Morris, George L. K.: *Industrial Landscape,* (oil, 63″ by 49″, 1950) Courtesy Downtown Gallery.

30 Mommer, Paul: *Studio Interior No. 2,* (oil on masonite, 30″ by 40″, 1951).

69 Murch, Walter: *Blocks,* (oil, 14″ by 22″, 1950) Owned by Arthur S. Brinkly Jr. Courtesy Betty Parsons Gallery.

52 Mullican, Lee: *Salt Fire,* (oil, 50″ by 45″, 1952) Collection Mr. and Mrs. H. de Schultheso, Courtesy Marion Willard Gallery.

20 Nelson, Carl G.: *Maine Night No. 2,* (oil, 50″ by 25″, 1951) Courtesy Boris Mirski Gallery.

94 O'Keefe, Georgia: *Early Spring Tree,* (oil, 30″ by 26″, 1950) Collection Dr. and Mrs. Joseph E. Gold, Courtesy The Downtown Gallery.

27 Oscar, Charles: *Night Journey,* (water color, 45″ by 42″) Courtesy the Downtown Gallery.

71 Ozenfant, Amédeé J.: *Building in a Park,* (oil, 60″ by 42″, 1950) Courtesy Ozenfant Art Center.

107 Perlin, Bernard: *The Jacket,* (oil, 1951) Courtesy The Art Institute of Chicago.

49 Pereira, I. Rice: *Ruby Flux,* (oil, 1952) Courtesy Durlacher Bros.

40 Peterson, Margaret: *Man's Child,* (oil, 43″ by 46¾″) Permanent Collection San Francisco Museum of Art, gift of Mrs. A. Mack and Mrs. A. Sals.

31 Picken, George: *East River Rooftops,* (oil, 30″ by 40″) Courtesy Frank K. M. Rehn Gallery.

62 Pollock, Jackson: *No. 12,* (oil, 1952) Private collection, Courtesy Sidney Janis Gallery.

39 Pousette-Dart, Nathaniel: *Renaissance,* (oil, 40″ by 48″ 1952) Courtesy Passedoit Gallery.

53 Pousette-Dart, Richard: *The Magnificent,* (oil, 86″ by 44″, 1950) Collection Whitney Museum of American Art, gift Ethel Schwabacker, Courtesy Betty Parsons Gallery.

105 Prestopino, Gregorio: *Roots,* (oil on canvas, 1952) Courtesy A.C.A. Gallery.

6 Rasmussen, Henry: *Involution in a Rocker,* (Duco, 30″ by 40″, 1951) Courtesy San Francisco Museum of Art.

57 Rattner, Abraham: *Farm Composition, No. 7,* (oil, 35″ by 46″, 1950) Owned by Paul Rosenberg Gallery.

102 Reinhardt, E. Ad: *No. 2,* (oil, 1951, 50″ by 80″) Courtesy Betty Parsons Gallery.

54 Reinhardt, Siegfried: *Sentinel,* (oil and wax, 36″ by 25″, 1950) Collection Sosenko-Hildegarde, Courtesy Whitney Museum of American Art.

74 Reinhardt, Marnye: *View into Maryland,* (oil, 1949-50) Collection Virginia Museum of Fine Arts.

38 Roesch, Kurt: *Walk in Town,* (oil, 50″ by 30″) Courtesy Pennsylvania Academy of the Fine

PAGE	ARTIST
	Arts and Curt Valentine Gallery.
97	Russell, Alfred: *Painting, No. 24,* (1950-51) Courtesy Peridot Gallery.
101	Ruvold, Felix: *Transcendental,* (oil, 72" by 50", 1952) Courtesy San Francisco Museum of Art and Catherine Viviano Gallery.
105	Salemme, Attillio: *The Sacrifice,* (oil, 60" by 80") Courtesy Whitney Museum of American Art and Saidenberg Gallery.
FACING 82	Shanker, Louis: *Abstract No. 1,* Courtesy Brooklyn Museum.
43	Schreckengost, Viktor: *Fish Forms,* (water color, 22" by 30", 1952) Collection J. Byers Hays, Courtesy The Cleveland Museum of Art.
101	Seligmann, Kurt: *Effervescence, No. 3,* (oil, 48¾" by 34", 1952) Courtesy Durlacker Brothers.
43	Sennhauser, John: *Synchroformic No. 27,* (oil, 36" by 4", 1952) Courtesy Artists Gallery.
58	Sears, Richard: *Towards Integrating Sculptural Influences,* (lacquer, 30" by 48", 1951) Courtesy San Francisco Museum of Art.
108	Shahn, Ben: *Compostion with Clarinets and Tin Horn,* (tempera, 36" by 48", 1950-51) Collection Detroit Institute of Art, Courtesy The Downtown Gallery.
37	Shanker, Louis: *No. 9,* (oil, 40" by 40", 1951) Collection Albright Art Gallery, courtesy Grace Borgenicht Gallery.
47	Shaw, Charles: *Tonal Rhapsody,* (oil, 22" by 30", 1952) Courtesy Passedoit Gallery.
28	Sheeler, Charles: *Manchester,* (oil, 22" by 28", 1949-50) Courtesy the Downtown Gallery.
19	Siporin, Mitchell: *Aging Actress,* (oil, 30" by 36", 1949-50) Collection Mr. Joseph Gersten, Courtesy the Downtown Gallery.
56	Sloan, John: *Riders in the Hills,* (oil and tempera on fabricated board, 19⅝" by 20") Collection Whitney Museum of American Art.
114	Solomon, Syd: *Boca* (polymer plastic, 32" by 44", 1952) Courtesy Sarasota Art Association and Harry Salpeter Gallery.
91	Spencer, Miles: *In Fairmount,* (oil, 42" by 65½", 1951) Collection The Downtown Gallery.
87	Spruce, Everett: *Precipice,* (oil, 24" by 30", 1949-50) Collection Daniel S. Defenbacker, Courtesy Fort Worth Art Center and Mortimer Levitt Gallery.
74	Stamos, Theodoros: *Death of the Anarchist,* (oil, 22" by 6') Collection Mr. and Mrs. John D. Rockefeller 3rd. Courtesy Betty Parsons Gallery.
2	Sterne, Hedda: *No. 32,* (oil, 44" by 31", 1952) Courtesy Betty Parsons Gallery.
72	Stevens, Edward John, Jr.: *The Red Bird,* (water color, 18" by 22", 1951) In private collection, Courtesy The Pennsylvania Academy of the Fine Arts and The Weyhe Gallery.
73	Stuart, Duncan R.: *Matrix,* (oil on canvas, 40" by 54", 1951) Collection North Carolina State Art Society and State Art Gallery.
25	Tam, Reuben: *Dark Wave,* (oil on canvas, 40" by 54") Collection of North Carolina State Art Society and State Art Gallery.
32	Tamayo, Rufino: *The Heavens,* (oil, 76" x 51", 1950) Courtesy M. Knoedler and Co., Inc.
111	Tanquy, Yves: *Suites Illimitees,* (oil) Collection The Pennsylvania Academy of the Fine Arts. Courtesy Pierre Matisse Gallery.
45	Tchelitchew, Pavel: *Revolving Head,* (gouache, 23½" by 20", 1951) Collection of Durlacher Brothers.
54	Treiman, Joyce: *Escape,* (oil on canvas, 1950) Collection of Art Institute of Chicago.
26	Thon, William: *Maine Granite Quarry,* (water color, 19½" by 40") Collection Mrs. A. Porter. Courtesy Midtown Gallery.
45	Tobey, Mark: *Orpheus,* (tempera, 22" by 16") Courtesy Seattle Art Museum.
78	Tooker, George: *The Subway,* (egg tempera on Masonite, 18" by 36", 1950) Collection Whitney Museum of American Art.
99	Tomlin, Bradley Walker: *No. 3,* Courtesy Betty Parsons Gallery.
23	Tworkov, Jack: *Sirens in Voice,* (oil, 54" by 45", 1951) Courtesy Egan Gallery.
41	Utter, Bror: *Pharmaceutic Cabinet,* (oil, 1952) Owner CIBA Pharmaceutical Products, Inc. Courtesy Dallas Museum of Fine Arts and Betty McLean Gallery.
81	Vytlacil, Vaclav: *Images of Pompeii,* (oil on board, 72" by 54", 1953) Collection The Pennsylvania Academy of the Fine Arts, Courtesy Feigl Gallery.
29	Von Wicht, John: *Harbor Festivity,* (oil and casein, 28¼" by 20¼", 1950) Courtesy Passedoit Gallery. Collection Whitney Museum of American Art.
109	Watkins, Franklin C.: *Beloved Dead,* (oil) Collection Arizona State College, Courtesy Frank K. M. Rehn Galleries.
88	Webber, Max: *Dauntless Bird,* (oil, 30" by 36") Courtesy Paul Rosenberg and Co.
42	Wigfall, Benjamin: *Chimneys,* (oil 1951) Collection of Virginia Museum of Fine Arts.
106	Wyeth, Andrew: *Man from Maine,* (egg tempera, 20" by 23") Collection Mr. Stephen Etnier, Courtesy M. Knoedler Galleries.
93	Xceron, Jean: *Painting 341,* (oil, 30" by 39", 1951) Courtesy Whitney Museum of American Art and Janis Gallery.
56	Zerbe, Karl: *Apartment No. 2,* (gouache, 25¼" by 18", 1951) Collection Downtown Gallery.